Stories from a[illegible]
Glob[illegible]
Volume One

Sharon Brown
(MO2VATE Magazine)

Published by The Book Chief Publishing House 2021
(a trademark under Lydian Group Ltd)
Suite 2A, Blackthorn House, St Paul's Square, Birmingham, B3 1RL
www.thebookchief.com

British Library Cataloging in Publication Date: A catalogue record for this book is available from the British Library.

Book Cover Design: Deearo Marketing
Editor: Laura Billingham
Coordinator: Nicola Matthews
Typesetting / Publishing: Sharon Brown
Proofreaders: Sharon Brown / Laura Billingham / Nicola Matthews

Table of Contents

Dedication

To all of the amazing women all over the world who are fighting some incredible battles and pushing through the toughest of challenges to create a life they love.

Foreword

By Emma Dunlop-Walters

The world is full of stories. Sometimes we get so busy we forget to stop and listen to the stories that make our world so great.

My journey into writing started because of MO2VATE Magazine. When I started my marketing career seven years ago, content writing was my weakness and over the years I have perfected the craft. However, I never believed I was good enough for anything I wrote to be in a magazine. When I came across MO2VATE, I decided to give it a go. I have written an article that I liked but was convinced it would go straight into the bin, so I was stunned when I received the email to say it was chosen for publication!

I didn't realise until this point that I was suffering from Imposter Syndrome when it came to writing. I didn't think my writing was good enough, yet here was an Editor who thought my article was good enough to be published.

I was published in April 2021 and this gave me the boost in confidence I needed to finally rid myself of imposter syndrome. I know my story isn't unique. MO2VATE has helped people with the same issue all over the world.

Each edition is full of advice, ideas and stories from people who would never have thought about writing or getting published.

Alongside the magazine, there are other writing projects on offer including this particular book, which I believe is an anthology.

Inside this book are stories that will inspire you and reassure you that anything is possible with hard work, determination and perseverance. I hope it inspires you to
think about the impact you have on the world and write your own story, maybe even in the next volume of this book.
To quote Matt Smith, "We are all stories in the end, ma ke yours a good one"

*****

FOREWORD

By Sarah Ross

It has only been six months since a post in a Facebook group brought MO2VATE Magazine into my life. What a six-months! A friend had recommended me for the Inspirational edition and I was thrilled to have my first article accepted.

Sharon Brown and the team made the process so easy, and more importantly in my opinion, fun! Each edition full of amazing stories and advice from a wide range of backgrounds and experiences. It's always a great read from start to finish.

In being introduced to MO2VATE Magazine, I found more than just an outlet to write for, I found family! Fellow Authors and the amazing team who were all striving for the same thing, to get the stories and wisdom that are in all of us, out to a much wider audience!

Thank you for all that you do and letting me be a part of it!

Introduction

This book highlights the life journeys of 21 inspirational women from different parts of the world, who have faced challenges that could easily have set them back in life, but instead they used their experiences to push themselves forward and create a life they choose.

We hope this book speaks to those who are currently going through challenges and allows them to realise there is light at the end of the tunnel. Persistence and determination and the sheer will to get through in whatever they choose is what has driven these Authors to where they are in life now and they want you to know, you can do it too.

Thank you for purchasing a copy of this book.

A CRUEL REALISATION
OF INDEPENDENCE

ABBI HEAD

THE VISUALS ADVISER

THEVISUALSADVISER.CO.UK

Chapter 1

A Cruel Realisation of Independence

By Abbi Head

As I picked up pace, striding down the street where I grew up, a life-changing realisation popped into my head with a sudden jolt. “I can keep on walking and never look back.”

Three weeks later I felt the resulting impact of this conclusion upon me, and it has defined my future.

Mum had always been worried that I would not cope if she died. I still want to tell her that in the process of me marching off that day, I had proved to myself that she had nothing to fear. I had supported her when she needed me for many years, despite all our differences. Just as she endeavoured to do for me. I simply did not realise that I had given her so much. However, I never got the chance to say, “Don’t worry, I’ll be okay now.” Three weeks after our argument, on 9th October 2020, Mum’s health deteriorated, and she passed away fighting against Covid-19.

Only two days earlier at 9.43pm she called me and the urgency she spoke with was immense. Her first words were, “I can’t breathe.”

I was not alarmed by the facts, but the instantaneous responsibility overwhelmed me.

I had shared her company only hours earlier, either disappearing into the kitchen to provide her with drinks and meals, or to watch a webinar on Facebook strategy. Mum was convinced that she was suffering from the effects of her flu vaccination. I repeatedly asked if she needed me to seek professional help for her. Bravely she refused.

My heart broke to offer her meals at arms-length, but I knew that we needed to adhere to social-distancing measures due to the pandemic, and she could not wear a mask. I had not hugged her since February, and I can still remember her smile as she stood at her front door on Mother's Day when I delivered her food and gift parcel. I tried not to be anxious and to make her laugh about our situation every time I visited, but this time it did not help, and I realised when it was time, that I was scared to leave her.

Now it was nearly 10 o'clock.

I immediately called an ambulance through sheer panic after her telephone call, but also because my words to Mum were, "What do you want me to do?".

I prayed she had heard the concern in my voice. It was difficult to process, but I jumped into the passenger seat of the car and we arrived just after the paramedics.

The reality began to creep over me like a windswept cloud blocking out the sun. Mum was in good spirits but did not respond how I had hoped. I know that she needed to be strong for herself, as she told one of the medics about her holiday cruise and her flu vaccination. She loved her cruises.

I spent my time trying not to cry whilst helping the second paramedic with Mum's medical records. I was relieved when the oxygen improved her symptoms mildly, however the paramedics suggested that she needed to be admitted to hospital. As she left, I watched Mum pass me in the hall, I felt a moment of freeze. I followed her to the ambulance and weakly said, "I love you", as she bravely sat inside. I do not know if she heard me. She was, in that moment, in every episode of my life both past and future. It was the final time I saw her.

I try not to think of the days that followed. My false hope when she was moved from Accident and Emergency to a Respiratory Ward seems naïve when I look back. I was awake through the night working on creative projects, hiding from the truth, and praying to something that kept me sane. This was an acidic test of resilience for all the family. When Mum's health deteriorated, she was admitted to intensive care.

I sensed her fragility and am haunted by the courage in her last words, "Tell them I will be watching over them." Mum always put others first before herself and this was often at her own expense.

As a family we visited the hospital as soon as we knew that we would ultimately be forced let her go. As I sat in the tiny room with my family the tears escaped revealing my powerless despair. I wanted to say, "No", when we were asked to reduce the oxygen that was keeping her alive. Mum had been placed into an induced coma because she had experienced a heart attack from which she could not recover.

I sank in my chair as it registered that the hospital ward was full of patients with Covid-19. The doctor felt my pain. I did not want to be exposed to coronavirus again. The doctor offered us all the choice to say goodbye to Mum, after all she was sleeping. "Think of the community that you are going back to," he said. I wondered what would happen if I contracted Covid-19 and whose life I might affect. That made my decision easier. Although it felt selfish, I said, "I can't."

My aunt was so much more heroic than me and she knew that she could self-isolate alone when she returned home.
Mum passed away within an hour of me leaving and my aunt was by her side. Mum had fought cancer and won. She had battled pneumonia and beaten it.

No matter what efforts we took as a family, it was Covid-19 that defeated Mum. Her hospital test results arrived later that day, and as suspected she had Covid-19. Suddenly every news story from March 2020, about families torn apart by a mystery virus, had infected mine too.

I would never be able to disassociate with this horrifying coronavirus pandemic.

As I write this, there is no immediate end in sight to the continued effects of Covid-19 in the world. The whole world is affected in some way, each of us have our own truth based on our environment and the information we have received. I understand that. Over the past months and into the new year of 2021, I have become desensitised to the mention of the pandemic and the lockdown because everyone talks about it daily. I am quietly listening and building resilience.

I found a voice in the middle of all the trauma and tragedy which I know I need to use. Mum used to call me "Little Voice", and she was so proud to know that she is featured in my public speaking and writing journey.

My emotions began to suffocate me on the day of my mother's funeral, and my words evaporated into irrelevance.

I spent weeks planning for this day as the restrictions had been lifted but then resumed. The funeral home raised me up as every step became more complex. As a family, we wanted a church service. We missed the timing. We would have liked to sing hymns. There was no singing aloud. Funeral cars for family members were impossible. Masks were to be always worn unless giving a reading of tributes and reflections. Everything we accomplished was a compromise and yet it was beautiful.

Mum's restricted funeral caused inconsolable grief. The gulf of space between the sixteen chairs set out for mourners at the cremation service isolated our lamentations into pockets. Prevented from giving my family a hug, the repression made me wince.

Throughout the service Mum's coffin lay directly in front of me and her photograph featured on a large screen. I needed to see her face. Her smile. Her happiness and carefree nature. I flickered my gaze between the two, while conversing with Mum in my thoughts.

Suddenly it was my time to speak.

My words began to strangle me as I read from a post on Facebook that Mum had shared. "The changes that I have seen in my lifetime and abided by have been unbelievable," she wrote, "You're never too old to learn..." I persisted despite the inner chaos.

Eventually I looked up through the blurred lenses of my reading glasses to see sixteen people focused on me, heads nodding. I felt as if I had channelled Mum into the room with us. I will never forget Mum as I morph into her more every day. A laugh. A phrase. Particularly every time I say, "As of", or "In a sense", when describing something. Her words are within my own thoughts and that comforts me.

Mum's Facebook post seemed to last forever, but I eventually completed it. I stopped. I exited the podium, sat down, took another look at Mum's coffin, and wept. I told myself to accept my vulnerability, reminding myself of the moment I walked down that street. Not through need, but I wanted her back. I miss her. It is so harsh to realise that our argument would enable me to face the reality of Mum's passing head on, realising my own independence.

Farewell Mum. Love you.

ALI FLEMING

HARMONY GLASS

HARMONYGLASS.CO.UK

Chapter 2

The Pain of Life

By Ali Fleming

Trudging up Highgate Hill, London, towards the Maternity unit of the Whittington Hospital on a blistering hot July day in 1982, I was heavily pregnant with my expected first-born child.

After attending many appointments with specialists and their moon charts, each time depicting a different date for arrival, there were two clear facts with my pregnancy. It was a breech baby - attempts to turn a 10lb expected weight around in the space was impossible. Not only was he/she big, but very long, and for a couple of months I had a perch of both head and feet side by side on which to rest my cup of tea - normal for me being my first pregnancy, but it caused a lot of interest in a teaching hospital. Surely it was going to be a caesarean section.

38 years ago, caesarean by epidural was a new phenomenon, and we would have been happy to have chosen that option - but somehow, they chose that I should have a natural birth.

How was I to know that it was quite "unusual" to have a breech birth by normal delivery. For all the medical students' (remember it is a teaching hospital) it would give a lot of gold stars to those fortunate to have the opportunity to observe. And boy they did! In a 12-hr. period I had at least 3 shift patterns worth, there might as well have been a television crew.

It was an extremely gruesome birth - not wishing to go into details, but my husband, a chef at the time, said he'd never seen anything so horrific, even with all the slabs of meat that he had jointed over the years! Joseph was born exactly 10lbs and at a length of 29cm, we knew long before his head appeared what sex he was, because he was born testicles first! That's another whole story. I will say that I went on to have another son - very similar weight but a much easier ride.

I want to share with you the image of carrying the ever-increasing weight of an 10lb baby on one hip, as you do for the first couple of years of a baby's life. And then add on 15 months later a 2nd pregnancy, almost as heavy, and balancing the two. I was made of strong stock, or so I thought.

Moving back to my own childhood, I was a middle child and had every syndrome to go along with it, I felt that right from a child, I just didn't fit.

My parents were busy, hardworking self- employed greengrocers, and I was primarily brought up by my maternal grandmother throughout my schooling years.

At an extremely young age, possibly from as early as 11 years old, I was expected to play my part in the business. I was dressed in a school uniform, but if I wanted anything "fancy", as my mother called it, then I had to earn it. I was introduced to the lifting of heavy boxes and bags of potatoes, cold, hard work standing on market stalls, my skeletal body was pushed to its limits even then.

My relationship with my Mother was volatile to say the least, and I think I was relieved when at 16 years of age I was thrown out to find my own way in life.

Years of feeling that I didn't belong, strengthened my thirst for being loved, and ultimately having my own family to love. At such a young age, being out in the wide world, affection was confusingly hidden by lust, and to be quite frank, males just wanting to have a good time. This led to loads more hurt, anger and disappointment, and at times deep depression about my own identity.

I did meet a wonderful man who I trusted implicitly and married when I was a young 21-year-old. That trust was to be broken again and again until everything snapped some 15 years later.

There is enough material to write a book of my life at this time, but the picture I am trying to paint here, is the damage to my physical (and mental) body.

By the time I was 36 years old, the next chapter was about to be written, as a single mum to my 2 boys, moving lock stock and barrel to Leicester for me to attend university, and the hopes of a new future.

The strain on my skeletal structure was showing, I was diagnosed with arthritis along my lower spine but predominantly in one of my hips. I was in agony, but continued pushing on, it was not in my plan to have time off for a hip operation. Regular visits to a consultant, who showed concern for the fact that my pelvis was being misaligned by my hobbling, then followed. Four years later, after graduating, I chose not to have a permanent life in a wheelchair and had an operation. A straightforward one, or so I was told. Had anything been straight forward in my life so far? No! I woke during the operation to hear my body being stapled up with a staple gun, things like that never leave you!

Although free of pain after the op, 12 months of physio was needed to try and straighten my pelvis and learn to walk correctly - straight and upright again.

Having often been described as a “troubled soul”, years of counselling followed in different forms, trying to come to terms with why I felt I didn’t belong anywhere, even as a mother myself.

I kept coming back with the same diagnostic message, a troubled relationship with a mother is a significant factor to physical pain and ailments, particularly in our skeletal area.

I was to meet and fall in love with my now husband of 17 years, he is a rock, a plodder maybe, but solid and never has any hidden agenda. He is 100% trustworthy and so supportive of me.

Six years ago, saw me jump into self-employment as a celebrant, two of the secure elements of working for someone else, are of course, the wage-packet every month, but also the knowledge that any time taken off sick is paid for, giving piece of mind for recovery. Two years into running my own business, I had to unexpectedly have my other hip replaced. The operation date was fixed for November, a quieter time for me for wedding ceremonies.

Preparing for the procedure, I had news that my father, living in Spain, was dying, diagnosed with terminal stomach cancer. He was sent home for palliative care and I spent a week by his side. The day I had my operation he passed away, I was unable to attend his funeral.

2019 was a successful year, bearing fruit from all of the hard work that had been poured into Cariad Personal Ceremonies, my celebrant business, but with that success, the physical elements became a problem once more. The driving, the sitting, the physical theatrics of delivering the ceremonies, and the lengthy amounts of standing. The pain was excruciating.

In the absence of my usual hospital consultant, I was offered an appointment with an alternative practitioner, who, after ordering fresh MRI scans and tests, put the whole thing into perspective for me. He talked in great detail about the birth of Joseph and the huge impact that trauma would have had, and has had, on my current health. The arthritis had spread at an alarming rate, and significant crumbling of my spine was highlighted, the condition was now permanent. Surgery could be an option but not in the short term.

There I had it, I was disabled. I was grateful for the "truth" and prognosis. Life moving forward (or not so much in my case) was going to be affected.

The COVID lockdown of this year was the reprieve that I needed. Time to think, to cry, to worry, to say "why me?". But out of the emotion came the strength, determination, the drive, and the innovation to launch "Harmony Glass". I still face the problems of being able to fulfil the number of ceremonies that have been postponed until next year, and have delegated many of them, others with rest, and dosed up with pain killers, I will deliver.

Remaining visible has been pivotal in my business moving forward, and after only a few months of launching "Harmony Glass", I was honoured to have been recognised for a networking business award. I also took to writing about my journey and was honoured to have been chosen as one of the inspirational women 2021 by Mo2vate Magazine.

Accepting disability is a challenge, it is unchartered waters for me, but I am not alone by any means, and I look upon it as another fresh challenging chapter for me moving forward.

ANDREA HOCHGATTERER

MIND BODY ALIGNMENT

MINDBODYALIGNMENT.CO.UK

Chapter 3

Guardian Angels and Knitting a Life

By Andrea Hochgatterer

Ouch, my ear, get off! I try and swat the pain away like an annoying fly. "She is coming round! Hello love, you are safe, and I am here to look after you, can you hear me? Can you open your eyes?"

I am trying to make sense of what is happening, my eyes are straining to focus, I can hear a lot of commotion around me, there are blurred noises and faces, I move to get up.

"Don't move, the ambulance will be here any minute now."

"Ambulance?" now I am confused. "I'm still here, not dead?"

"What's your name love?"

"Andrea"

"You are still alive Angela; you must have a Guardian Angel."

"Andrea", I mutter resentfully.

“It is a miracle you did not crash through the windscreen seeing you did not have your seatbelt on.”

They lift me into the ambulance.

“I don’t want to go to hospital, I am fine, I’ll walk home.”

“Sorry Angela, no can do, you have to be checked over first. You are in shock, just breathe deeply”.

The oxygen mask goes on. “Breathe? Ha, ha, very funny!” I am getting angry, I want to scream and fight off their attention, when suddenly memory comes flooding back, or better, is hitting me hard, as I sit there, blankets wrapped around me. I start shaking like my life is depending on it, and it probably is with all the adrenalin inside me, and I can’t stop the images coming.

Half an hour earlier…

Easter weekend in Vienna, I have accepted a lift from a neighbour into town for a quick Easter egg shopping spree, before catching the train for a rare visit to my family living 200 miles away. The guy driving is talking a mile a minute, telling me all about his amazing new car, and hitting the new fast circular around the outskirts of the city, he really puts his foot down whilst still talking and constantly looking at me. Was I impressed enough with his car’s prowess, suitably in awe of his driving skills? “What does he want?” I am not really interested but keep nodding politely when suddenly my stomach lurches.

I spot the little red car cutting across, jumping the light, my foot is already on the imaginary brake whilst simultaneously realising Mr. Talkative is not going to slow down, he is looking at me...we are not going to make it, I'm dead.

My life starts flashing before my eyes, "just as it is in films", I think in wonderment,

I say goodbye to all my friends and family, sorry for not staying around, sorry for not delivering the Easter presents, sorry for being unreliable and the hassle my death will be causing, sorry for all the things I will not be able to do now.

With a heightened sense of awareness, the world starts looking like a shrill version of a Van Gogh painting, the glittering midday sun, the brilliant blue sky, bright yellow and green daffodils cutting through the snow, I feel elated light and weightless.

A screeching of brakes, my body curls itself into a tight ball in an attempt to save my life.

"Goodbye me, goodbye world!"

They jab me with something, I eventually stop shaking, and what seems like hours later I can finally go home. I stay with a friend recuperating from concussion, cracked ribs and patella's, bruising, and minor injuries, nothing more, which everybody tells me borders on the miraculous. Guardian Angels are being mentioned again.

The trouble is, I don't feel alive.

I know, supposedly I am in shock. Everybody tells me it's normal to feel dazed and quite disconnected, but I just can't shake the feeling that I have died. I appreciate solicitous friends, and concerned doctors offering tranquillisers, antidepressants, painkillers, and a friendly pat on the hand, "there, there, you'll be fine!" happily releasing me back into society. Family expects me to snap back into shape and get on with it, but I am far from over it.

Back in my own little flat, well enough to look after myself, I expect to go back to Uni and finish my degree, however I can't. I can't think straight, don't want to even continue, in fact I don't know anything at all, I don't even know who or what I am any longer. Did I feel angry, deprived, sorry for myself, poor me…of course I did, all that and then some. I blamed everybody, the drivers, the cars, myself and the stupid seat belt, God, and the Universe for punishing me.

"Why me?" Inevitably and eventually like a shockwave it hits me: what if this was meant to be? What if this car accident was meant to happen to stop me in my tracks, what if the so-called Guardian Angel did not so much save my life but literally crashed me to save me?

I lock myself away, this needs thinking about, I need space.

Despite cries of woe from concerned friends, I refuse any contact, I refuse to just snap back because I really have to figure this out by myself with the help of my own four walls and the cheese plant as company.

That is when I find a long-forgotten basket of wool, a never finished project, and start knitting and thinking and thinking and knitting.

The click clack rhythm of the needles, the flowing of wool, the colours of the sky, trees, sun, emotions, thoughts, are all taking on shapes and patterns. Threads of cotton, sheep's wool, silks, strands of frayed fabric, interwoven are knitting new stories, my nerves calm, understanding is dawning. I experience an influx of incredible dreams and stories which I don't understand at all, and which seemingly have nothing to do with me (turns out to be snippets of past lives...but this would be another story).

My brain feels like it is uploading stuff, or maybe something is downloading into it, who knows, I can see my childhood through a different lens, I can feel and sense events in a different light, consciousness is expanding, and, though this might sound strange, a little voice in the back of my head keeps nagging me. "I recognise this, I knew this as a child", that's what I was thinking when I was little looking at the grown-up world around me. "You have got it wrong! This is not how life should be!"

Working away incessantly my life comes back into focus, the fog starts lifting and I perceive a thread running through my life, the carrying of others, steadily supporting, and making peace to avoid conflict, being quiet and compliant to always accommodate others, not taking up too much space, not getting in anybody's way, always taking NO for an answer because my life depended on it.

So, my big dreams of becoming an artist, being creative in the theatre, designing clothes…oh the list of my ideas was endless; one way or another were laughed off, ridiculed, swept neatly and cleanly under the carpet and magically disappeared in a puff of smoke. I ended up with the sensible and very cerebral option of studying marketing, advertising, and psychology. I am not pointing the finger of blame at anyone, it is just how things were in those days.

I resurface and three months later I have a collection of knitted creations. I start off by wearing them myself, people stop me in the street, wanting to buy them, wear them, the word spreads and I continue for the next four years to create and expand. My take on country inspired cotton jerkins turns out to be a hit, and even start selling in Paris. I move into silk designs and the same thing happens, until one day life takes a turn again; this time I follow the thread effortlessly in the deep conviction that I can trust myself.

As I bring my story to completion, I suddenly realise that this happened exactly forty years ago. I am so grateful our society as a whole has come a long way with improved knowledge and acceptance of ACE, PTSD or even Near-Death Experiences, being able to provide effective support to those out there who need it.

Has it all been plain sailing for me since then? Of course not, which is just how it's meant to be. I believe we are here to live and learn at all times, to grow as individuals and to follow our hearts without having to make excuses. I can advise you with great conviction to never give up, whatever happens, don't take no for an answer, you have the strength and knowledge within yourself to follow your dreams, however unlikely it might seem that they will ever come to fruition.

If anybody tells you, "not a chance in the world", don't believe them!

ANDREA A SMITH

ANDREA A SMITH

ANDREAASMITH.COM

Chapter 4

The Power Within You

By Andrea A Smith

Stress, which has been constant, simmering under the surface, has affected all areas of my life. Feeling stressed for an extended time seems ‘normal’, because you lose your reference frame between what stress feels like, and how being calm feels. Awareness of your stress can work for or against you, you understand what changes you want, but are you ready to make them? Understand how to open your mind to the power of change within you, allowing you to seek new ways to make changes and take back control.

I had to accept my self-sabotaging behaviour and develop an ‘I can, and I will', attitude. This set off a chain reaction within me. I am now thinking positively (even though it's a struggle at times) and behaving in a manner that works for me, and not against me.

How my journey began:
About 14 years ago I found myself in New Zealand, abandoned by my husband. He was having an affair while the children and I immigrated to his home country. I found my way back to the UK and started all over again as a single mother of two children.

There were tears, fears, exhaustion, together with stress and anxiety, how would I cope? Being human, I wanted to throw in the towel, yet something stopped me. I had two innocent children that depended on me. I felt angry, frustrated, scared, fearful, anxious, and stressed, all rolled together into one big emotion ball.

Everyone wonders about their path in life: what they "should" be doing, where they belong, and with whom? I was in the same situation and wanted to find answers. There is a knowledge of who you are, an understanding of your power and path encoded within your memories.

Not acknowledging these memories, to know yourself in depth, is like choosing to remain a stranger to yourself. I have met many people who speak about wanting to do certain things, I can hear what they are saying from a place of deep longing - the type of longing that comes from wanting to know oneself.

With the challenges of being a single parent, I was busy and had no time for self-reflection. I could not work full time as a nurse due to my children's needs, so I worked as a part-time agency nurse. I had the responsibility of bringing up two children without any support network. I struggled with stress and anxiety and did not know what to do and where to seek help.

Facing my challenges:

Even though I worked part-time as a nurse, from a medical perspective I noticed that people were unable to get to the crux of why they struggled with anxiety and depression. As a nurse, I cared for many people suffering physical ailments, who were also struggling with stress and anxiety (like me). They were on pills and drugs that deadened them even more inside. Working as a nurse, giving them medication, and not getting to the root cause of their problems, left me feeling powerless. Let me share the case of a young woman who came to the hospital after a miscarriage. She was devastated and felt ashamed as this was her second miscarriage. She was worried that her partner would leave her due to the loss. She was depressed and very anxious but hid her pain and was on a massive dose of antidepressants. She would not talk about it as if she opened up, she would have to deal with the loss. She tried to speak positively, but the pain was apparent on her face.

I felt helpless, but knew that I could help her and people like us who struggled with stress and anxiety. After all, I was not relying on pills to help with my anxiety, I was able to feel better. And If I could, so could they. Many people struggle, do not know what not to do or how to feel better. It was not enough for me to watch people struggle with no support, except the basic help from an overstretched system (NHS). Moreover, it could take three months before they could have an appropriate counselling appointment.

From my personal experience, I knew there was a better way. Determined to understand the human mind, I decided to embark on a Master's degree in Psychology.

It seemed the more exhausted I felt, the more committed I was to change my life for the better. I saw this great opportunity of making a difference by helping people struggling with stress and anxiety, as I had overcome my struggles. I was not content with completing my Master's in Psychology, I went on and studied many more tools. Strategies to help me work with people to change their lives for the better from the inside out. With my story as the evidence of what is possible, proof of such transformation.

"*Be the change you want to see in the world*", Mahatma Gandhi - a statement I am seeing and hearing more and more often. It is one of the many principles that guide me in my life's work of helping people to get to know their inner struggles and explore their inner world so they can consciously reconnect with all that they indeed are. This brings me back to my quote. When we have an attitude of curiosity and interest, with a non-judgmental acceptance of whatever we notice, then so much more becomes noticeable, more apparent, as it is not disregarded. So many possibilities open up to us.

I found the resilience, confidence, motivation, and strength inside me, even when I thought it did not exist.

I found what it was like to be me, and was surprised how I had rebuilt my life brick by brick. When I came back to the UK, I knew I had to be strong: I had to work two jobs and bring up the kids by myself.

I went back to university part-time and finished my second degree. And then, a couple of years later, I did my Master's in Psychology. I was amazed at the energy I had, juggling it all. I was proud of myself, and my children were doing great at school.

I built myself and my business from scratch. The next few years was involved learning marketing and business skills, how to run my business, networking with businesses and people around me. I learnt to be genuine, authentic, and true to myself, serving my clients to the best of my ability.

My relationship breakdown experience, being a single mother and having to rebuild my life has been my catalyst.

Creating a new path:

As my confidence grew, I learned what I wanted and drilled down into my 'why'. I found that I had a deep knowledge and a comprehensive understanding of medically and psychologically why people were struggling.

Stress resilience coaching is my passion, creating a new path, empowering others by showing them how I empowered myself. A recent Kings college study with 3000 adults showed 57% reports symptoms of anxiety, and 64% reported common signs of depression.

Furthermore, I had grown in so much knowledge, expertise, and confidence I decided to bring my journey and philosophy together and authored my first book, 'Fear Less, Live More". It was the icing on the cake. I am very proud of the book. My signature programmes are built around the book so that people can use them in their daily lives.

Perceptional Change: Most people work on their physical diet, but how can we manage our emotional one? When you ruminate, feel fearful, anxious, worrying about contracting Covid 19, struggling with the feelings of loneliness, and lack positive thinking, this can impact you emotionally. What is the answer, and how can you feel better, happier and make the changes you desire in your life?

Perceptional change is having practical ideas for change, positive thoughts and reframing the negativity you feel.

Recent research found that 80% of all illnesses are linked to stress impacting our immune systems and compromising our health long term. This can cause long term damage to your physical health - like cancers etc. We need a healthy immune system.

Perception change means building resilience. If we let all the adversities in our life break us down physically and emotionally, we will not become stronger with life's experiences.

Reframing means 'how you respond'. To me, this is the key to building resilience. Even if the pressure over time builds up - you can control how you respond and perceive that pressure. It's not only your bounce-backability, it is your capacity to bend back to your centre. Flexible enough not to let the cracks with life's challenges break you.

"*We all have, and have had, hard knocks - truly gutting ones - yet many do not speak of them, they are busy making a new life. Do like-wise.*" Clarissa Pinkola Estes. The last 12 months have been stressful with this pandemic. 'Fear Less, Live More', my first book can help you with your struggles. Stress and anxiety cannot win, you can find happiness and freedom. Focus your mind on the things you want and discover the power within you. **You can do this**.

ANITA ANDOR

ANITA ANDOR

ANITAANDOR.COM

Chapter 5

My Biggest Loss Gave Me Purpose

By Anita Andor

I grew up in a loving and warm family in a small Hungarian town. I considered myself a lucky child with easy-going parents, not being pressured too much. Of course, there were the occasional motivational speeches about how great it would be if I studied to be either an economist, a doctor, or a lawyer. My grandparents had the same thoughts about my future.

My adolescent years were an internal struggle for me from an educational perspective. I did not see the value in learning many subjects and refused to read mandatory novels, yet I still marched through primary and secondary education with above average results.
During these years, I was daydreaming a lot. I imagined living in a big city, working with "fine" people while spinning around in an office chair and enjoying the skyscraper view. Oh, and wearing those pairs of red stilettos! In conformity to my mother's tales, it was neither my intention to hide nor to keep my thoughts to myself.

Being an extrovert and a chatterbox, I often voiced who I wanted to be when I grew up. I recall those worry free days playing with pretend rotary phones posing as an estate agent. The biggest treasure of my childhood was the feeling of effortless joy and wholeness. I did not feel the need to have a purpose to feel happy and whole. I just existed, and it was OK. I trusted the journey and was glad to be here.

At sixteen, I got into the wrong crowd, became a rebel, did not intend to go near any university, and was kicked out from a two-year course I'd enrolled in just to get a qualification to make my family proud.

I found working in a bar for long hours more amusing than studying something that did not interest me at all. From sixteen onwards, I was spinning around like a ball on a roulette wheel, except that I stopped at the same position every time - a club. My drive to achieve my dreams was lost, like money lost on playing roulette. I was in denial. I believed and convinced myself that I was innocently having fun, although deep down, I knew I was running away from reality. I felt helpless not knowing my truth, and I should know it, right? At least, that is what my ego screamed to my higher self.

Twenty-two years later, I discovered that I was escaping the feeling of being lost and being ambitionless. I could not accept myself without direction and a plan.

I thought I was less, not good enough, without knowing and doing what I envisioned for my future - a future created by my inner child.

In secondary school, one of the subjects that grabbed my attention was the English language. At nineteen, I packed my bags and came to London to learn English and endeavoured to get out of the emotional whirlpool I was in.

London captivated me, but my hopes for bouncing forward was nowhere near close. The first ten years were memorable for partying, confusion, no purpose, studying and working in a field that I secretly found boring and disliked, and living someone else's life. The feelings were all too familiar, and slowly I stopped trusting my journey. I was a mess; I developed gut, hormonal, and skin issues along with an emotional battle that I am still working on today. I had no idea who I am, and why I am here. Do not get me wrong; I am not complaining. Eventually, I landed an Advanced Diploma in Finance and Accounting, I enjoyed the skyscraper view and relentlessly wore my red stilettos, but those dreams were no longer meaningful.

Everyone has their own fears and demons; I believe mine is not having a purpose and feeling lost. It feels empty inside. It was at this low point I started playing with the idea of changing my mindset, my crowd, finding a hobby, and getting myself out of the victim mentality I built over the years.

I started off with my physical health and stopped partying.

Then when I was thirty-two, my father was diagnosed with pancreatic cancer. I still remember the day and how that day changed my future. Despite feeling severely nauseated and broken, I put on a brave and positive shield, and I deep-dived into research on cancer and holistic health, hoping to save him without using harsh orthodox treatments. I was introduced to a book that changed my perspective of the human body for many lifetimes to come. It equipped me with the knowledge to truly understand what the human body is capable of provided it is given the right conditions.

I prepared personalised meal plans with high-quality supplements and followed the same protocol so that dad did not feel left out. The next four months were challenging, heart-breaking, and painful. Let me say that I was daddy's girl, and so watching my strong father turning into someone that resembled a skeleton, was making me angry and even more determined to bring him back to the man he was.

While the doctors praised us for having good lab readings, sadly, cancer had won after four months of extensive suffering. He passed away in our hands at home, the day after we had told him it “is OK to go”.

Besides feeling like a punching bag, a rash of blame and guilt moved into my heart. All those years I spent partying and abusing my body and mind could have been spent with my father. That is all I could think about. For some time, I became a bitter and introverted person. I was jealous of friends who still had a father and got closer to people who had lost their fathers. I was only capable of and wanted to identify with pain. There was no joy such as those childhood ones. In fact, there was no joy at all in my life for some months. But one thing that I did not give up on, and even did more of, was learning about nutrition and health.

Initially, I was thinking to change my career and work with cancer patients to honour my father and reduce the incidence of this horrible disease. But I did not have the strength to go ahead with it. I had to be honest with myself. I was not resilient enough to work with people who reminded me of my father passing.

Seeing him suffering and being so fragile was an eye-opener for me. I made my own health a priority and treated my body and mind with respect. Human physiology and nutrition, how our bodies should feel when nourished and energised, and emotional health became the centre of my focus.

Two and a half years later, I was free of all of my health struggles. As a result, my mindset, energy, and principles took a hundred and eighty degree turn.

I enrolled to study naturopathic nutrition at the College of Naturopathic Medicine in London. During the three-year course, I also developed a strong desire to grow as a person, and read many different books to grasp how to find that inner peace I was so longing for. I had regular acupuncture sessions, ate super healthy, and felt resilient. I was happy and full of joy, just like my inner child. My mission and purpose were born. That is to educate and help others be the best version of themselves, and show up for them during the hard moments. That is a purpose worth living for!

Today, my belief is that health, resilience, success, happiness, confidence, and joy, are only available to me if I continuously support my body and mind. I have not met a single person, including myself, who can honestly say they have perfect health. It just does not exist in this day and age.

I neglected to look at my health for longer than it should be allowed, and I hope my story inspires you to take action now. You may be surprised and find the purpose and peace you are searching for. It is in all of us; we just need to breathe and feel a bit deeper. Failing, learning, wanting, loving, laughing, and pain, are all part of the journey. Our job is to respond and embrace every aspect of it.

Ironically, the loss of my father gave me my purpose and transformed me into a healthy and strong woman. I choose to thrive, and I choose to grow every day.

Dad, I am forever grateful for that!

With Love,
Anita Andor

ANNA GOODWIN

ANNA GOODWIN ACCOUNTANCY

ANNAGOODWINACCOUNTANCY.CO.UK

Chapter 6

Learning to Adapt and Thrive

By Anna Goodwin

I remember sitting in a classroom in France when I was five years old, not even understanding how to ask to go to the toilet. The smell that was always all-pervading was couscous. A terrible shock for a child used to English food. I still don't like the smell and don't eat it.

Mom was a French teacher and she had taken the opportunity of exchanging with a French teacher who taught English. They came to Bloxwich and we went to Aix-en-Provence in the South of France. 'We', included me and my sister, Mary, who was seven, and my brother, Will, who was nine.

It was like being catapulted into a new world. Everything was different! Of course, the weather was a nice change from what we had experienced in the West Midlands, and we played outside a lot more than we did at home.

It didn't take long for us to learn the language, and once we had, we continued speaking French, even when we were playing together on our own. It certainly helped being one of three siblings, as we had each other.

There were many positives of living in France for the year. It was a once-in-a-lifetime experience that most people haven't had. We could go to a river with friends - which we did regularly - and have great excitement playing, wetting the rocks and sliding into the water. Fun times! Because we lived there and my mom made friends, we were invited to other houses and experienced how the French people lived. Some of it was good - some not so good. I remember feeling sick when told that the rabbit stew contained the rabbit we had been playing with last time we had visited. However, most of the time I enjoyed the way they all ate together, taking time over their food, laughing, and telling stories.

When we returned home once our year was over, we went back to France each year for the six-week holidays. It was fantastic to be able to spend time on the beaches near Saint Raphael and drive out to the Carnival in Nice. It always felt natural to go back. It seemed like going home. I have spoken to my sister about this, and she feels the same.

Looking back, it feels as though we had adapted so well to living there that it didn't feel right to be going back to the UK. This must be a problem for parents who decide to return home after an exchange year. They know they are going back to friends and family and this is what they want to do. Children, especially at the age we were, haven't yet made solid friends and their family is mainly confined to their parents. For them, in many ways, it would be easier and healthier to stay in the new country.

In the intervening years when our annual trips ended, I hadn't really thought about France and using my French. But on a holiday in Majorca when I was 30, I met up with a Swiss guy and started chatting in French. I once again realised how much I enjoyed the language. Not long after that holiday I decided to use my French at work. It was a skill, up until then, that I had taken for granted and not made the links to the benefits it could give me in my working life.

Being able to speak French enabled me to work in London and France. When working all over France I never felt scared or lacking in confidence. Knowing that I had coped when I was only five gave me additional courage - if I could do it then, why couldn't I do it now? If I didn't know the word, I didn't panic, as I'd experienced it all before.

Working in France was a fantastic experience, both personally and for my business skills. I carried out one-day audits of universities and Chambers of Commerce to check that they had used their European Commission grants correctly. I grew into myself and finally grew up. Having to get eleven French people to do what you want them to do in a meeting does that for you! Also, travelling on my own around France - whether by train, plane or in a car - was a great experience and taught me to become independent and focused on where I was going.

Having worked in London in an employed capacity, using my French influenced my self-employed work. From regularly working in a different language, I knew that I didn't want to specialise and enjoyed the variety of having many different clients. The receptionist at Moore Stephens would often phone me to say they couldn't make out the name of a person. I would know that any minute I would have the opportunity to speak French. I liked that spontaneity and having to think on my feet. It is something that I value today, and I continue to do this now in helping clients with their issues and jointly coming up with solutions.

When I meet people who have moved their family abroad, I'm always interested if it's been a success or not. And if it has been a success, how they managed and how they overcame any problems. One family I spoke to said that their youngest had found it difficult to fit in at school. The older children of a campsite owner seemed bored and isolated. When I spoke to them, I realised we'd been lucky, as once we'd recovered from the shock, we all fitted in like ducks to water. For us, it was coming back and having to readjust to the UK that was a struggle.

There were many downsides of having lived in France for those 12 months. I never felt like I fitted in at school when we returned. In fact, when Mary and I were first back at school in the UK, we continued to speak in French!

I yearned to live in France and always felt at home there when I returned. To the extent that I never made much effort to make friends at school as I always thought we would eventually go back.

The year had an impact on my schooling as I didn't pick up the basics in say, maths, in the same way as I would had I been in the UK, as we were taught in French and taught the French way.

It's funny how experience affects us in different ways. My brother loved it and says it was a fantastic time for him. I think as he was older, he coped better. For me, being on my own at school and unable to speak the language (even though this was only initially) scarred me, and I believe led to my school phobia when I was eight. And even now, I always have to take some kind of snack with me when I am going out because not being able to ask for food in France left me worried about going hungry.

It was only later in life that I could see the benefits of my experience and this gave me the confidence to make the jump into doing work I love. When I reflect on my French connection, I realise the experiences that shape our lives are not always obvious in the benefits they bring until many years later.

Even though it finally impacted on my life in a positive way, I wouldn't do it again or encourage anyone else to do it, as I never felt the same about the UK afterwards.

However, I made a conscious decision to focus on the positives that I'd gained and use them in my career. This then helped me realise that I loved being placed on the spot. I loved thinking on my feet and problem solving and this is exactly what I ended up doing.

When I think back on it now as an adult, that five-year-old girl was so brave. It was a big upheaval for her! It was an experience that taught me a lot; some good, some bad.

The good include:

- Living outside more
- Experiencing how French people lived
- Learning to think on my feet

The bad include:

- The impact on my schooling
- Never feeling like I belonged in the UK

Working in France when I was older dispelled the idea of moving to France, as I realised how fundamentally different they are to us. In particular their sense of humour! It obviously wasn't meant to happen anyway as my hearing isn't very good now. I can still speak French with a good accent, but when they reply I miss what they are saying.

Although I would not want to go through this again in life, I'm grateful for what I gained and how it had an impact later in life.

ANNIE GIBBINS

ANNIE GIBBINS

ANNIEGIBBINS.COM

Chapter 7

Twins Twice to CEO

By Annie Gibbins

Women are powerful. Something overlooked by so many. Mothers often give this power away, not just to their children, but to others.

We forget to look after ourselves, we forget to dream, and we forget to embrace the strength and capacity to achieve the extraordinary.

When I became pregnant with my first set of twins at 23 years of age, I was in shock, but excitedly so. When my second set of twins came just two years later, the shock was laced with elements of fear, overwhelm, and a sense of "How am I going to do this?"

I was, and still am, blessed with an incredibly supportive husband who has always been involved with every aspect of our children's lives. We navigated the uncertainties, the challenges, and the sleepless nights together. We always have done, and it is this united front that has helped me get through the days and nights when I forgot who I was; especially when our fifth child came to bless our family five years after our second set of twins.

As mothers, we tend to take on a lot of the responsibility of parenting and raising children ourselves, but we don't need to. Whoever we are, regardless of our family formation, we always have people we can turn to. I had my husband, but I didn't have my mother or siblings. Other women have their siblings or friendly neighbours but no partner. The local mother's group is a great place to start building a support network, but you have to be willing to ask for help.

A few years after my children were born, I remember crying and asking my husband, "Is this my life now? Is this it? There has to be more to my life." I wanted to be more than just a mum, more than a milk machine, more than just a zombie of sleepless nights and babbling conversations, of nappies, vaccinations, and percentile growth. I felt like I was going crazy!

And whilst being 'just a mum' may seem unkind to the women who choose to be a stay-at-home mum, that wasn't who I was born to be. I was born to lead my children in a different way. I was born to lead women in a different way. I was born to run my own business and make a vast difference to people around the world. But where would that dream fit in? Where would I find the time for me? What would I do with the children while I was studying and working? Would I be able to cope with the extra workload? Thankfully, I got curious and started getting creative. If there was one thing being a mum of five children taught me, it is that empowering attributes are worth fostering.

Finances were tough, so getting creative with clothing, days out and holidays was necessary. I found you can actually do a lot without very much when you really put your mind to it. Adding to the pressure, I had a strong desire to go back to university but had no cash set aside for an expensive MBA. So, over the next few years I set aside two evenings a week to study a Master of Education, and eventually the day arrived, and I graduated.

My crazy dream had been realised. My options expanded greatly. My self-belief grew strong and my dreams grew bolder. I realised that my curious nature was on my side. While others doubted my abilities or criticised my choices, I was thankful that my inner voice dared to ask, "What if…?" So as my children grew, so did my curiosity and creativity in finding new ways of finding my essence. Being Annie was enough. Being our authentic self is always enough as this is who we're born to be.

Being a mother equips us to become excellent project managers. We develop skills in logistics, negotiation, and financial planning. Whilst navigating years of sleep deprivation, we learn to problem solve while juggling multiple balls in the middle of separating fighting toddlers and cooking dinner. We spend years developing high level managerial skills, but they are often overlooked by society. As mothers, we sometimes overlook them ourselves.

If we undervalue ourselves as women, we don't learn to ask for what we actually want.

The problem is some of us don't even know what we want. When our children repeatedly ask us for something, and we ask them what they want they say, "I don't know, I just want something." This answer frustrates us, especially if we are busy - but we do exactly the same! We know we want something different, something more than we have now, but we don't give ourselves the time to simply be on our own to find out. We feel guilty for spending money on ourselves, because 'Little Johnny' needs to go to after school clubs, or 'Little Janey' needs to attend ballet classes, but in reality, it is our choice to fill our days with afterschool activities. For some, it can be a subconscious way of avoiding having that time to focus on their individual wants.

Our children do not need all the things we think they need, nor do they want all the things they say they want. What children really need is a mother who is energised, happy and fulfilled in life.

Pioneering women, including my own grandmothers, have challenged the long-held narrative that men have the right to be more, achieve more and earn more, and in doing so have paved the way for the women of today to step into a more empowered future.

Madam C J, a black woman who created a hair care and cosmetics company in the early 1900's, chose to say no to this narrative and became one of the richest women in history. Coco Channel chose to create her own future, her own income and live life on her own terms through fashion. Political leaders like Margaret Thatcher and Eleanor Roosevelt took the political arena by storm, and Michelle Obama and Adriana Huffington are currently fanning the flame for women to believe they can thrive in their unique circumstances.

All these women had a burning passion to make life better for them and their children. They had a dream, and they went for it. They stood up to men and challenged social programming. They threw caution to the wind to make their dreams come true, regardless of how tough it was for them.

The next generation of women play an important part in shaping the future. In order to achieve this, young girls must be supported and empowered to know they are capable of anything, have access to every opportunity and most importantly, demand more for themselves. It's time we focus on the next generation of talent and make sure gender equality exists for the good of everyone.

Growing up, I never had someone who I saw as a role model, other than my father, who was my rock. I never had a person who I wanted to emulate or be like. I wanted to be me, so my curiosity around who I was, helped me to create opportunities to learn and grow.

By doing so, I became happier, more fulfilled, and more successful.

Making time for myself gave my husband precious time with the children. It also taught them that parents should not forget their essence, even when they adopt the centrepiece of the family.

My children have grown up watching me study, get curious about what's next and become a hugely successful woman. This has taught them that anything is possible, regardless of which gender they are, whether they have children, or how many children they have. It has also taught them to be respectful of other people's time, become self-reliant and choose for themselves who they wish to be.

Becoming a mother of two sets of twins and then a beautiful bonus 5 years later, never held me back. It was the challenge I needed to become the Annie I am today. It has led me to become a role model for women globally, and now with a biography available about my journey into 'Becoming Annie', and my latest book, 'Twins', which showcases the very best of becoming a parent of twins twice, I am able to reach more people around the world. I help them realise that becoming a mother doesn't mean what others tell you. It is an opportunity for you to discover your own version of motherhood.

Motherhood isn't an easy journey by any stretch of the imagination. It is a very enjoyable one, and incredibly rewarding, provided you never forget yourself in the process of caring for others. You are YOU first and foremost.

BRENDA DEMPSEY

BOOK BRILLIANCE PUBLISHING

BOOKBRILLIANCEPUBLISHING.COM

Chapter 8

Evolving Purpose

By Brenda Dempsey

Many people go throughout their lives trying to find their purpose. They question: "Who am I? Why am I here? What should I be doing to help others and make me happy?"

I too have asked these questions from an unconscious place during my lifetime. But my curiosity came from a very different place from the conscious place I now live. I used to live from desire, which in itself is an okay place to start.

How do you eat an elephant? One bite at a time.

When I was a child, I had an overwhelming desire to become a teacher. At that time I was not sure why, except that I loved school and learning. At home you would often find me playing at schools, and of course I was the teacher. I would love to play at schools to show off my maths skills or spelling, but most of all I loved reading stories and asking questions.

The social aspect of school was great, and I was a popular girl. I was sporty and no one could catch me, so I was picked to do the chasing in team games because I was fast.

I was a typical girl playing ring games such as 'My girl's a Corker', 'The Big Ship Sails through the ally ally Oh', and my favourite, 'The farmer wants a wife.' Many playtimes were spent swapping 'scraps' - beautiful cut out images of children, angels and flowers - trying to get whole families or getting rid of your less favourite ones.

School was my purpose in life in my early years, as early as primary. How do I know? Well I was the one who took new pupils under my wing. I was always looking out for the child who no one wanted to play with. I had this strange feeling that it was my responsibility to make sure they were alright. Perhaps it was the nurturing mother in me. I found myself standing up for the child that was teased. I refrain from using the word 'bully' because in the 1960s it was not a word I heard in school.

Have you ever experienced a curve ball from left field? Well that is what happened to me. For someone who loved school so much, at the age of 16 I found myself leaving it without a single qualification. That choice closed one door but opened another and as someone who loves life, I made the most of that situation too. It seemed when I make a decision, good things follow.

At the tender age of 17 I found myself married, and by 21 had my first child. I went on and had three more children and by the age of 29 my family was complete. Of course being a mother means being a teacher, so my innate desire to teach and help others be the best version of themselves continued. This time my students were my children. As a mother I only wanted the best for them, so I had to give the best of me.

It wasn't too long into motherhood that I found myself having an active part in my community. As a new mum in the early 1980s there were not many groups for young mothers, consequently in good Brenda fashion, I decided I would start one. Before long, the head of the nursery school approached me to ask if I would be interested in being the parent representative for a new idea of creating a multi-disciplinary team to support parents. You guessed it, I jumped at the opportunity. Here was little old me, without any educational qualifications being asked to be part of an innovative idea. I was to be part of a team of education, health, social services, and community whose focus was services for Under 5s.

Needless to say the next ten years were spent in schools serving them as a Parent Teacher Representative, parent helper, and taking my children's school netball team practices. I was in heaven.

The desire to become a teacher grew stronger. But lurking in the back of my mind was that I did not have any qualifications, in fact I didn't think I was smart enough, even though something within told me this was not my truth.

I developed good relationships with the teachers, especially the young head teacher who encouraged me to consider going to university and studying to become a teacher. How, I asked myself? I am a mum of four children! That seemed a huge mountain to climb. Not only that I have no qualifications. During one conversation, she told me about a scheme that helped mature students get back into learning. Ah - a window of opportunity. Dare I grab it? Of course I did.

It was not a case of worrying about the 'how' but focusing on the end result. At that time I had never heard of Stephen Covey, never mind 'begin with the end in mind', something that serves me well today and that education has taught me. I was giddy, excited and the thought of realising a life-long dream motivated me to the max. This was intrinsic motivation at its finest. I will never forget the wise words of this young head teacher. She said to me, "Brenda, you will only get out of life what you put into it." At first her words did not register, but when they did, BOOM! It was after all my mantra in life - 'Love it. Live it!' Words I often find myself sharing with others too, even 'til this day.

I spent the next five years training to be a teacher. I loved every minute of it. I also found the old competitive spirit of my athletic past re-emerged. I wanted to be the best, do my best, and give my best, and I did, despite the hell I lived through during this time.

I always knew I was a determined person; I had enough experience to strengthen my belief in that aspect of me. I always believed 'I CAN', yet on occasions I would doubt myself, only to realise I could find a way of making it work, whatever that would be.

On 28th October 1996, after five tough years, I graduated. With the exception of the birth of my four children, it is my standout moment in life. I was floating on air. I had achieved something that meant the world to me. I was not stupid as some people had led me to believe, because, in the deep red tube, was the paper that stated otherwise, I was a fully-fledged primary teacher.

Armed with my degree, I soon found myself standing at the front of a classroom with thirty odd children staring at me. WOW, what a feeling. I leapt into action and loved every minute of it, watching those little faces light up, lightbulb moments occurring, and lapping up the sounds and smells of school. I did have a moment and thought, nothing changes, the sounds and smells were exactly the same as when I was a child who sat excitedly hanging onto every word of my teachers.

After three years of supply work I found myself with a permanent job. The universe had conspired for me to be in the right place, at the right time and knowing the right people.

The field of Special Educational Needs was calling. I was always being head hunted for my teaching prowess. The children loved me, they were achieving great results, and most of all I had a knack of behaviour control. My kids were always the best class in school. I believe that is down to my respect for them, giving them my best and encouraging them to do the same. It worked and I used this strategy throughout my career; after all it is how I lived my life.

I was living the dream when the second devastation in my life happened (the first being my failed marriage) - my father died, followed by my mum one year later. Again the universe was my redeemer. I had met someone and found myself leaving my beloved Scotland and travelling south of the border to settle down in Surrey, England.

It was easy to get a job, and before the summer holidays were over, I had a job in a Special School for children with Autism. I loved it. I grew, and after eight years I found myself changing school for a greater leadership role in a large secondary school, running a special unit for autistic children. I loved that role too, but a change of leadership caused my world to crash around me.

I found myself on the self-development path due to my interests, opportunities, and leadership training. Like a death, I fell out of love with my role but not with teaching. In January 2006, I left my beloved teaching career to take up the baton of entrepreneurship.

I look back over my deep desire to be a teacher, and realise this is my purpose in life, no matter how it shows up and presents itself to me. If you look at your life, there is one common thread. I also believe you have more than one purpose in life, and when you are aligned with who you were born to be, the universe will not disappoint, and the opportunities will abound as each door opens. The question is, 'Are you brave enough to walk through?'

CERI GRIFFITHS

WILLOWBROOK LIFESTYLE
FINANCIAL PLANNING

WILLOWBROOKLFP.CO.UK

Chapter 9

Ego to Empathy

By Ceri Griffiths

Embracing your kindness, your empathy, your softer side allows you to win on a whole new level.

But do you know what may be getting in your way?
Your ego.

What is your ego telling you about what success looks like, and have you checked in with this lately?

Checking in with my ego led me to leave a highly successful corporate career, and to start on a whole new, more aligned path.

Early Days

My ego had been with me from childhood. A pivotal moment in my teen years, when a teacher remarked that if the girls were to go to home economics, there would be more room for the boys, steered the direction of my life for the next 20 years.

Whilst I experienced more joy with English and languages and art, I was able to do well in Maths and Science. I chose them because they were "harder", and I would be proving more by doing them. I did a Maths degree and pursued a financial services career for this very reason.

I didn't value the strengths I have that didn't fit my ego.

I spent a corporate career chasing success on this basis. The need to be seen and heard, to be as good as the men in the room. To use my ego to drive forward.

Realisation

But as I got older, as my career progressed, I started to love certain aspects of what I did more than other parts, and I noticed men around me didn't seem to value them in the same way. My compassion, empathy, my communication skills were not in the job description.

I realised how much of the other stuff I did bored me, and that scared me a lot.

I didn't feel right – but I didn't know why.

At this stage in my career, I was a coach and mentor to other financial advisers. One day I was observing an adviser in a meeting with his clients, and I caught the eye of the female client and it hit me, she felt the same as me.

Intuition

I knew something wasn't right, but I didn't have the language to express it. It felt physical, uncomfortable. It felt like a duty, something I had to address.

I didn't truly know what my ego was, or how it was showing up, and there was no one around me who was bringing this to the table.

I hadn't met other women who had taken any sort of a different path to me, and so seeing anything outside of my narrow vision was hard.

But it became an itch I had to scratch.

Perspective

I had the chance to be professionally coached, and it was a game changer. When faced with what I truly valued, and what I really wanted my life to represent, I knew I had so much more I should be bringing to the table.

And I learned about energies.

I grew to understand that I was working in my male energy. Constantly pushing, striving. Constant ego and not in touch with my feminine energy.

These energies are prevalent in Chinese medical theory, where "Yin" refers to the feminine energies in life, and "Yang" to the masculine.

Giving is an action of our divine masculine and receiving is an action of our divine feminine, and a balance of both is when we feel harmonious.

Now this isn't about gender, these energies are universal, we are all born with Yin and Yang energies and we all have the potential to lean more towards one or the other.

What I recognised is that there had been two decades of being in Yang.

Two decades of ego.

I had pushed my Yang much to the detriment of my Yin. And I no longer was aligned to who I wanted to be.

The Seed Was Sown

I started to think about how I could realign.

I thought more and more about how the female clients I observed interacted with their money, with their adviser, with financial services.

I began to plan what a business designed for women like me would look like.

There would be no egos.

It would engage and inspire women by talking about what they value, not about "beating the market" or jargon.

It would be human, with real connection where the discussion about money was about how it needed to work to align with our values, needs and hopes.

It would balance the Yang, with the very much missing Yin.

Being Brave

Starting Willow Brook is hands down the bravest thing I have ever done.

To step out of a successful career and start a company so out of sync with what everyone else was doing was terrifying, but in my gut, I just knew it was right.

Learning to trust my intuition has been priceless, as has having the clarity and perspective to realise I am a feminist.

Equality is not sameness. Being different to a man does not make us weaker. The differences should be embraced. What both parties bring to the table is valuable.

We need the Yin with our Yang.

What has been the hardest part? Being brave enough to show my empathy. To show up with kindness, with authenticity and vulnerability. It is common to have one vision of success, and to step back and review what I truly felt, where I really added value, to really assess who I was, was tough.

But it's been absolutely the part that has made the difference.

<u>Inspiring Others</u>

Social media has allowed me to shake off the austere and corporate image of financial services, and to talk about financial planning on a human level.

But more than this, it's made it easier for women to reach out and get the advice they need, because instead of feeling intimidated by a big corporate image, they know they are reaching out to someone just like them.

It has allowed me to help women not see money as a bore and a chore.

The product focus, emphasis on growth and discussions around economies are the traditional Yang element of financial services that makes it so very hard for women to find them inspiring.

But when that narrative is switched, when the discussion becomes about what you want and need your money to do for you to build the life you want to live, then women can find themselves truly engaging.

My vision is a future where women find it easy and attractive to be money savvy.

Embracing Feminine Energy

Meditation and journaling for me are key in embracing my feminine energy.

If I find myself driven with a constant to do list, then I know my Yang energy may be in overdrive. Balancing this with days for creativity, days to reflect, and days to meditate and journal help me with reaching harmony.

Adapting my routine this way has made me more effective, not less. Instead of feeling like I need to be constantly achieving, crossing off actions, I now recognise the value of Yin, how time spent in pause is valuable and adds to the overall direction and momentum in ways I could never achieve if I ignored.

It has meant being brave. Taking a step into it. Listening to my body and my soul.

Walking into My Story

I love this Brenne Brown quote; "When we have the courage to walk into our story and own it, we get to write the ending".

I know that my story is owned. It's not perfect, but it's true, and I embrace that.

Have you walked into your story?

How will you write the ending?

Mine is with empathy and kindness, and with the inspiration to help others.

Removing the ego was the best thing I ever did.
Yin AND Yang.

EVERYTHING HAPPENS AT
THE RIGHT TIME

ELKE WALLACE

MASTERING YOUR MIND MATTERS

EAWALLACE.COM

Chapter 10

Everything Happens at the Right Time

By Elke Wallace

Have you ever felt you were born in the wrong country? I was born in Stuttgart, Germany, as the last of four children of Bavarian and Sudeten-German originated parents. My siblings were ten plus years older and loved the music of the late 60s and 70s, which mostly had English lyrics. I loved the sound of the language and preferred the music to what my parents enjoyed, which was a mix of Oldies, German Schlager and especially the dreaded Volksmusik (oom-pah bands, yodelling and the likes).

My Mum taught me English words she remembered from her school years. I loved watching things to do with Britain on TV, like the weddings of Princess Anne in 1973 and Charles and Diana in 1981, or Black Beauty and Follyfoot.

I felt strangely drawn to the UK, and the English language that I started studying properly from age 10 onwards at school. It was one of my favourite subjects with my best grades.

After the school years, English was sadly not part of my apprenticeship at the District Court in Stuttgart, but I continued language studies in my free time. And earning my own money enabled me to put savings aside to make plans for visiting Britain. One of my friends from the apprenticeship class wanted to go to London, so we got planning and I booked a trip for July 1986 just after the main apprenticeship finished.

On 7 July 1986 we waited to board the delayed plane at Stuttgart airport, sitting on those orange plastic seats with my stomach in knots due to excitement. The evening sun was shining through the large windows and there was a massive rain shower, which created one of the most colourful rainbows, as we went to board that Dan Air aircraft to Gatwick.

Have you ever been to a place and felt it was your home? Walking the streets of London's West End and beyond, had a strong feel of déjà vu to it, I felt as if I had been there before, as if I had come home. My friend and I spent a fabulous two weeks in the capital, including a visit to a festival in Basildon, where we sat on the grass, chatting to Vince and Andy of Erasure before and after their gig.

When we went back home, I knew I would be back soon. I knew that two-week trip was only the beginning.

I visited London again in summer 1987 with my best friend Liane, having this premonition of a fire at Kings Cross as we looked at the ancient wooden escalators - the Kings Cross fire happened in December that year. The following year, my UK trip included day trips to Brighton, York and Liverpool while staying with an older lady in Catford, who took in students.

The more I visited, the more familiar I got with the country, even more so after travelling to Scotland as well from 1989 onwards. But how would it be possible to move and live there?

From 1990 I worked for the District Council of Cologne after moving there. It was a civil service job with no requirement of English language skills, and no possible option for any job transfer. Things looked hopeless, but I didn't give up on my dream. During my time in Cologne, I got hold of some information about moving to the UK with all basic requirements. I studied these documents very carefully and decided I wanted to move in 1994.

Which did not happen.

Instead, I completed another English language course with Chamber of Commerce and Industry certification and started applying for jobs in the private economy in the Frankfurt/Main area with companies like Proctor & Gamble and the big German banks.

Job hunting in the private economy was difficult for a visually impaired person with albinism, who had no university degree or A-Level education and only work experience in the civil service. I found the interviewers quite judgemental, like the one at Proctor & Gamble on her high horse asking, “Why did you not attend university?”

Then I spotted the ad of a small company in the financial services industry looking for a Junior Secretary in Spring 1995. I secured the interview in Frankfurt. The boss was curious about my health condition but in a friendly way. She was very welcoming and non-judgemental. Long story short: I got the job, moved to the area in June and started work in Frankfurt in July.

The job was a step into the right direction!

The company had their European headquarters in London and the main headquarters in Glenwood Springs, Colorado, USA. My colleagues were such a great lively team, and the best part was - English was the main language of communications with all international offices, of which there were quite a few. I fitted in well, learned my tasks very quickly and got more and more things delegated to me, and I visited London for training many times. And my German and UK colleagues gradually learned about my plans to leave Germany in 1998, come what may.

I had no idea then what was coming.

In July 1997, I spent my holidays in Britain again for three weeks, starting with friends in Tunbridge Wells before travelling to Scotland and finishing for a last stopover with my Tunbridge Wells friends prior to flying back home.

It was mid-July. I stayed at my favourite B&B in Fort William. After being out and about on this hot and sunny summer day, I went to a phone box in town to call Tracy, the Billing Supervisor at the London office, to check if we were going to meet up as intended when I was back down south. I dialed the number and she said unfortunately something had come up, so we sadly could not meet. However, she said, she had a proposition for me. "We know you want to live in the UK. I have been talking to Brian (the London and Europe boss). We decided to restructure the Billing Department, and if you want you can have a job in Billing."

I was gobsmacked! My stomach nearly jumped out of my mouth. I asked Tracy if I had heard right, which she confirmed. She then suggested I think it over and I could give her my final decision once I was back in Germany. This was it - it would happen at last. I would leave Germany for good!

Of course, I accepted the job offer once I was back home despite having no idea how to find a place to live. I had a job to start in November, but what about a home?

While I considered my options, a London colleague, Judy, told me about her friend Wendy, who had bought a new home in Woking and was looking for a lodger. Her move was scheduled for October. This sounded ideal. I didn't mind being a lodger, at least I would have a place to live. It looked like things were finally falling into place. Judy had told Wendy about me and was put in touch with me. We arranged details for visiting her in her new home after her move-in date, and only weeks before leaving I visited Wendy in her little cottage home in Woking. I ended up meeting her whole family and little dog Ozzie.

Everyone warmly welcomed me, I felt at home right from the start. Wendy was happy for me to become her lodger, so after discussing arrangements for my move I went back home, safe in the knowledge I now had living quarters.

My Frankfurt colleagues were sad about me leaving, but they were also happy for me that I could realise my dream of emigration.

The last two weeks were extremely stressful.
First, I had to find a new tenant for my rented flat. It is customary in Germany to find a new tenant to secure the continuation of tenancy for the landlord, which was a greedy company in my case. I cannot even remember how or where I found a guy who wanted to rent the flat, but I somehow did.

I also had to arrange a removal company for the relocation of the possessions I could take with me. My siblings came to take over some of my furniture, while other pieces were to be left with the new person. And work was extremely busy at the time as well, with a first client event coming up that needed arranging for the end of October.

Finally, the 2 November 1997 arrived.

I anxiously waited for the new tenant to get his keys, all packed and ready with the remaining luggage to get my lift to the airport. The guy eventually turned up, my things got packed in the car and off I went to Frankfurt airport and checked in.

After patiently waiting, I got on the plane - it was time to leave.

My dream had come true at last.

EMMA DUNLOP-WALTERS

E R MARKETING

ER-MARKETING.CO.UK

Chapter 11

Starting a Business During a Pandemic

By Emma Dunlop-Walters

To look back at Christmas 2019, it feels like a lifetime ago. Looking back it is hard to believe how much the world has changed since then. The things we took for granted were suddenly gone and insecurity was all around us. I got married in November 2019 and we started 2020 feeling secure and on track to meet our personal goals. Then COVID-19 hit and changed everything.

The virus raged in China, yet we felt secure it would never come here, we believed it would soon disappear and be a bad memory. With March came the first national lockdown and the end of our world as we knew it. This virus was deadly, and it was on our doorstep.

There was hope that the lockdown would kill the virus, that in a few weeks we'd all go back to normal. During this time I was working in a marketing role, and I was really struggling to adapt to working from home, it felt strange to not be going out every day and the furthest I moved was from the sofa to the bedroom.

By the end of March I got the news I was being furloughed, which wasn't a surprise as most companies were using the Government scheme.

I tried to stay positive and used my new found free time to do some volunteering and start working in a part time care assistant role for a local care agency.

The weeks went by and the virus was showing no signs of stopping anytime soon, but getting out of the house and doing something productive was good for my mental health, which had taken a decline since the pandemic began.

June came around, and I received the news that I had been expecting, I was being made redundant from my marketing role. As I had only been in my job for 8 months there would be no redundancy money. All we had was my husband's student loan and the wages from my 16 hour a week care job which was ending in two days. I didn't have a plan, everything was spiralling out of control and so I shut myself off from the world.

I ignored messages from my friends who wanted to make sure I was OK. When I did answer, their attempts to cheer me up failed, so I didn't answer the phone. I barely moved from the sofa and depression sank in. The care agency offered to extend my contract, but I needed a break, everything had hit me so suddenly I just wanted to hide away from the world.

My career that I had worked so hard for was in tatters, I was scared of losing our flat and everything we had worked so hard for. Because of something that wasn't in my control.

On 5 July I got ready for my last shift with the care agency. I wanted it to be over so I could get back to the sofa and wallow, but that one care visit changed everything.

My final client that day was one of my favourites, she had worked hard and had achieved so much in her life. I told her what had happened, and she looked me right in the eye and said "well, what are you going to do?"

Before I even thought about it, I said, "I am going to start a marketing agency." The words hung in the air and I stood there open-mouthed. I had thought about getting some freelance work but there was no way I was good enough to run a business, I had no business experience. Yet I had said it, the words had come out of my mouth.

My client looked at me and smiled. "I know you can do it, so go do it." She looked at me right in the eyes and said with a stern smile, "Don't let me down". Then she started laughing and enquiring about my plans, to which I answered as best I could, seeing as I had just made the plan.

I went home and started putting my plan together, my husband built a website and we started building the foundations of a business. I hardly slept during the first few weeks, and self-care went out of the window. I lived, breathed, and slept the business.

Those early days were scary, exciting, stressful, and yet I felt like I was on the right path. The fear of failure followed me everywhere but so did the determination to make it work and change our lives. I wanted to come out of this with two things - a thriving business and my mental health intact.

Everyone told me that my working pattern wasn't healthy, and looking back now I can see that they were right. But I was fighting off depression, trying to run a business and keep everything else running while coping with a constantly changing world caused by COVID-19. I struggled to take breaks from working which meant I ended up working 14 hour days 7 days a week. When I did take a break, I felt like I was failing - my attitude was that every waking hour should be dedicated to the business and nothing else mattered.

Over time I managed to build up a network of experienced business owners who guided me along the way and offered me a lot of advice in the early days. But the one piece of advice I refused to take was to take a break every now and then. This led to burnout.

Burnout

Balancing a part-time job and running the business got too much for me but I still didn't stop. It had been an intense few months and I hadn't spent one moment of it doing something that wasn't about the business. I felt like the world was on my shoulders, I was running a business with no business experience and it was hard.

I pushed these feelings aside and carried on because I felt like if I stopped for a break then the business would fail, and I would have nothing. I was stuck in this cycle of negative thoughts and depression but couldn't face dealing with my feelings, so I carried on.

A few weeks later one of my business contacts emailed me and said he was training to be a life coach. As part of his training he needed to take on some clients to practice with, so he asked me if I would be willing to help him.

I said yes, but then started thinking about other people I could offer this too because I didn't need it. Everyone I talked to about it insisted that I take the opportunity, looking back they probably saw what I didn't - I needed help.

Our first session came around and after he had explained how the session would work, he asked what I wanted to talk about and I said I was fine, everything was fine.

Then he asked me what was going on in my life and before I knew it, I was crying. I felt shame for crying but when he said that I needed to let it out, I did for about twenty minutes. I listed off a lot of things that I didn't even realise were bothering me, I had bottled everything up for so long and now it was all coming out.

The life coaching sessions not only changed my personal life, it also changed the way I ran my business. By the 8th session I felt tougher and felt confident in myself, and I believed that I could do anything. His main piece of advice was to take a break every few days, I had heard this so many times over the last few months, but I decided to try it and see what happened.

I gave myself a few days to not think about the business and focused on myself, for the first time in months.

After my break, I got back to work, and my business soared. Only this time, I wasn't working 14 hour days 7 days a week, my coach taught me how to challenge negative thoughts and how to not be so hard on myself.

I learnt to make myself and self-care a priority, and that the world wasn't going to end because I took an evening off.

I started my business in the toughest of times, during a pandemic when the country was on its knees. Looking back at the journey I have taken still makes me emotional.

The main lesson I learnt was that anything is possible with determination, hard work and dedication. For anyone who ends up in a similar situation to me, believe in yourself, remember that you can do anything you set your mind to. But be kind to yourself along the way, starting a business is a very tough journey.

KIM LENGLING

KIM LENGLING
KIMLENGLINGAUTHOR.COM

Chapter 12

Let Fear Bounce

By Kim Lengling

Fear. That nefarious four-letter word has the power to creep up on you and derail you.

I've experienced fear in many forms, as many of you have. I've learned over the years to recognise it for what it is, acknowledge it and kick it to the curb.

You know what I am talking about. Self-worth, depression, anxiety, and more.

As a veteran who lives with PTSD due to sexual assault, for years I let fear creep into my days as well as my sleeping hours. Stealing peace and rest. Stealing joy and self-worth.

Once I recognised it for what it was, I worked to relegate it to where it belonged. In the garbage.

Has it been an easy journey? No.

Some days are tougher than others. We all have them. It is in how we choose to deal with them that matters, it is our choice in how we want to feel.

Let me share with you a story of the type of day that can slither in on a day in the life of a woman with PTSD.

You may be able to lock it away in a room in your mind, but as time goes by and life happens, the door to that room will crack open. As it opens wider, all manner of thoughts and feelings may rush at you from every direction.

This may happen at night while you are trying to sleep, or it can happen during the day, sneaking up on you. Your breath becomes shallow and you become hyper-aware of your surroundings.

Rationally, you know that you are okay. You know that you are in a normal setting, and as that darkness continues to settle around you and the heaviness weighs down upon your shoulders; it has the power to bring you to your knees.

You fight the weight of the darkness. You do your best to focus. What do you see? What do you hear? You must try hard to focus. Your hands' clench and muscles tense.

Breathe. Smile. Do not let anyone see what you are going through. You have become a master at disguising all that is going on within your mind and body. Take a deep breath and look around, people are standing in groups having normal conversations, no threat. Focus, listen. Ah, there it is, you hear music. You know the song and softly hum along with it.

Move forward. Keep that smile on your face. There you go, you got through that one. This may happen occasionally, or it can happen daily when you least expect it. The effort that it takes to keep control is so very tiring at times, and yet sleep is elusive. You know when you fall asleep, dreams will come, and in those dreams, you will fight another battle.

Dawn arrives. You have slept for three hours. It is the start of another day. Do not look in the mirror. If you look in your own eyes, you will see the tiredness and the sadness that lies within.

You are alone. There is a storm within you. You often wonder if there is an anchor out there somewhere. A person who does not fear the storm but is willing to chase it. One who is willing to be present.

You question your worth. You see yourself as weak. You cry out to God. You believe, but does he hear?

The storm settles. You have done it; you have made it through another day. No one chooses to have PTSD. A traumatic event occurs in your life and alters your life and how you view the world.

It becomes a part of you and you of it. It is an invisible scar. It is exhausting, and yet, each person who lives with PTSD is a warrior fighting battles no one sees. There is tremendous strength in that. Make no mistake, there is strength in that.

Is this an everyday occurrence? No, it is not, yet those days can, and do, creep in.

I firmly believe that the world and personal circumstances play a large part in how our subconscious mind recognises and deals with things.

The world has changed drastically. That change ushered in new fears for many. I made myself a promise to let fear bounce. That was a phrase that came to me one day and I have used it for over a year now. I use it for myself and share it with others. We can't live our daily lives in fear. We weren't meant to live that way. We are made to live and prosper while caring for one another. Showing kindness, love, and compassion to each other.

How can I or you let fear bounce? For myself, I take my past experiences and put them into words, verbal or written. There is power in sharing your story; power to heal, to embrace, to encourage, and to provide hope. I can't think of any reason why I would not want to provide any of those things to someone struggling.

Each time I share my story with someone, a small piece of the weight falls away from my shoulders. Not only that, it shines as a small light for someone who may be sitting in darkness. Letting them know that they too can weather the storm and come out stronger for it.

Struggle and trials may come for just that purpose. So that we can overcome and be a person who provides hope and encouragement to someone else.

I have accomplished more than I anticipated or was able to see, once I realised that I can be a light for someone using the written and spoken word.

I am a multi-published author, a freelance writer, podcast host, and speaker. I am a mother, a friend, a shoulder to lean on when it is needed, and ears to listen when someone needs to let go of some of their darkness. It comes naturally to me as I know what it feels like to be in a place where you feel alone and unable to cope.

Empathy. I have become strongly empathetic over the years. That in itself can be tiring, yet I welcome it. It is a gift that I embrace, as I can listen to someone, or at times look at a person, and feel the heaviness they carry. I can feel a hurting soul and want to reach out and help.

That help can come in many forms. A smile at a stranger. Recognising and acknowledging that someone is hurting. I may not always be able to fix their problems or assist in their struggle, but I can acknowledge their hurt and let them know that I see them. I feel for them. They are not invisible, and they are not alone, no matter how heavy that solitude may feel to them.

When is the last time you acknowledged someone hurting? Did you offer to help or at the very least, offer a hand or a hug?

Human connection is so important, and yet with the world the way it is at this point, fear holds people back from showing compassion and empathy. Fear is holding people back from letting the human side show, all of it hidden behind masks, and the dark, heavy days become more prevalent for many.

If the human connection is closed off to me for now, I shall continue to write and share the spoken word, to send out kindness and goodness into this broken, frightening world.

I am on a mission. I want to toss small pebbles of kindness out into the world, one word or one story at a time. There is power in kindness and power in words. Don't let fear hold you back from sharing that power and potentially changing someone's world.

I may not change the entire world, but I can change one person's world one written, or spoken story at a time.

What will you do to make the world a better place? What will you do to make one person's world a better place? We should all strive to let fear bounce and be a beacon to the world. A light of kindness, caring, compassion, empathy, and love. It maybe you on the receiving end of it.

KYLIE ANDERSON

KYLIE ANDERSON COACHING

KYLIEANDERSONCOACHING.COM

Chapter 13

Fulfilment on the Road Less Travelled

By Kylie Anderson

I met my childhood sweetheart at the age of 16. I knew he was the one for me. It was comfortable, fun, and easy. He was a good friend of my brother and I knew he was a good fish.

We built a house together and moved in. I was after that dream relationship. I had a wonderful childhood, with two amazing parents and a loving brother. I was happily on track to settle down and have children. How wrong I was! Personal tragedy struck just a few short years later.

I'd just spent the most romantic weekend away with my partner, in a lovely cottage up in the wine country. We returned to my family home full of excitement and plans for the future, to share with my parents the news that we had just got engaged.

Six years together and he'd finally asked me to marry him. I was so excited and on top of the world.

We saw the police car drive out of my parents' home and I joked with my partner, "What's he done now?" I was talking about my brother Scott, who had a habit of getting into fairly harmless trouble in his decked out cars.

All I remember is walking into the house, looking at my mother and her turning to me and telling me that Scott was dead.

I've never forgotten the look on my mum's face. But the devastation that followed is impossible to even comprehend.

It was all a bit of a blur from then on. We had to drive over to the hospital to identify his body.

We'd found out that my wonderful brother had been in a motorbike accident, with a car that was on the wrong side of the road. First, I felt anger, and then profound shock. I was still young and couldn't really comprehend what was going on.

Soon after, we found that he'd done everything he could to survive. He threw his bike under the car and he went the other way. But it was a country road, and unfortunately he landed on one, innocent rock. A rock that took his life. It ruptured his spleen. He was too far out and by the time the ambulance arrived, and they airlifted him to hospital, it was too late.

Life can change in a moment.

Following this devastating loss, at just 21 years old - when I should have been the happiest ever - I learnt the hard way that life was very precious.

Ever since, I've lived with the motto, "Life is too short so make the most of it".

Life soon moves on, but it was never the same again. You feel like you are just going through the motions. I shut down a bit and put up some barriers. But my partner was really patient with me and we made it through.

We got married a couple of years later, but we divorced in under 12 months. I thought we were happy and about to start a family. But then he came home one day and said I don't love you anymore - and left. He had started seeing a lady that had been hitting on him at work - my so-called friend!

Those few years were full of pain and rejection. I lost myself and fell into a bad relationship.

But I do thank the universe now, as when I look back, I totally realised my awful ex-partner was just there to get me through the pain of losing my brother. Sometimes people come into your life for a reason. Sometimes they stay and sometimes they don't!

"Many people walk in and out of your life, but only true friends will leave footprints in your heart."
Eleanor Roosevelt.

Just 6 years later, when I came out of the bathroom and realised for the second time that I wasn't pregnant, when all I wanted to be was a mum, I knew it was time to shake things up.

I had been in a relationship with my existing partner for just over 4 years, but I wasn't really happy, and I saw this as a sign.

Maybe the universe was trying to tell me something!
It was time to do something totally different. So I booked my first ever trip overseas.

The excitement of getting on that plane made my heart sing!

My first big trip was a 30-day adventure around Europe on a bus. It was full of party animals, but I was more interested in seeing the sights and experiencing the cultures. But what it did give me was a taste for different places - we did 12 countries in 21 days and saw some of the biggest landmarks - like the Eiffel Tower in Paris, Leaning Tower of Pisa in Italy, the amazing canals of Venice and so on.

This was just the beginning of my amazing travel journey. I now live in the UK and have been to over 45 different countries. I love new experiences, the people you meet and the fun that happens on each journey.

One of my favourite trips was travelling through Africa. I spent two unforgettable months, firstly on a group overland trip from Nairobi down to Victoria Falls, seeing the wild animals of the Serengeti, meeting the Masaai and enjoying the spices and beaches of Zanzibar.

Then travelling by car with a good friend along the beautiful coast of South Africa to Cape Town.

Travel broadened my horizons and opened my eyes to a bigger and wider world. It also empowered me to be more and develop my strength as a woman. I often travelled alone, joining random groups, and stepping outside of my comfort zone, which developed my other gift of not being afraid and created my ability to talk to anybody anywhere.

But it wasn't all good fun. Of course to feed the travel bug I also had to fund it!

That meant working hard in the corporate world. I carved out a niche as a very successful Sales Manager with a multi-million pound department in a busy West London Estate Agency. I loved it, but at the same time, I was getting burnt out. I soon found that even though I was earning loads of money, I wasn't doing the things I loved anymore, including travel!

Time was ticking away. I was getting older and my body clock was going off again. I was feeling the pressure of my friends around me all settling down, having kids, and wondering why I wasn't. The amount of times I was rudely asked, "Why don't you have kids, what's wrong with you?" I remember being at a good friend's barbecue surrounded by "smug" couples who were judging me because I didn't have children.

I knew they assumed that I was a failure in life.

That in some way I wasn't good enough to be a mum. There was something wrong with me.

Why hadn't it happened for me?

I also felt guilt that I had somehow let my parents down. They wanted to be grandparents, to see me happy and settled down.

It wasn't until I turned 40 that I really started to reflect on my life and on where I wanted to go in the future. I realised there was a burning desire deep down in me to do something different. I just didn't know what. Looking at my boss one day I realised I didn't want to be him in five years' time - and that made me take a step forward. I knew then it was my time to step up and make a difference.

So I started my entrepreneurial journey, which as we all know isn't really about business but about personal development. Through highs and lows I've built a successful online coaching business and created the freedom to work from anywhere, fulfil my passion for travel and be able to spend my time between Australia and the UK with family and friends.

This was my healing time, the time to really let go of the guilt and to accept the path I had chosen (well the universe kind of played a part!).

I found out, after doing a few therapy sessions that took me into a past life regression, that I had already had two wonderful lives with big, amazing families, and that this time around I wasn't meant to have kids, my soul had something else in mind.

This was the last turning point to letting go of the feeling of failure and really stepping into my path. My path to help others to take their expertise to create a bigger impact.

I know deep inside me that I am here to make a difference.

I just wasn't meant to do it the traditional way.

So, I've focused on what I truly believe, "If good women earn good money, they do good things with it…"

My message - Expert Impact is growing and helping other service-based professionals to share their gifts online, so they go on to create a bigger impact. I like to call it the "ripple effect".

I do this through a simple, yet highly effective, 4-Pillar Process that allows service-based experts, like coaches, therapists, property professionals and so on, to create, launch and scale an online signature program.

This not only creates additional income (one of my clients went onto create 6+ figures last year with just one product) but more freedom in their business and a way to create their own personal impact.

Expert Impact consists of 4 Key Pillars:
PILLAR 1 - PLAN
PILLAR 2 - PACKAGE
PILLAR 3 - PROMOTE
PILLAR 4 - PROFIT
My firm belief is that if you INCREASE YOUR INCOME you INCREASE YOUR IMPACT.

And the best bit is that you can do this too.

I wanted to share this with you, to inspire you to realise your own dreams.

I've embraced my life, the road less travelled. To explore the world, to meet new people and to grow my business dreams.

It's time as women, we step up and believe we deserve more. We are worth more and we can have whatever we want. The only limitation is our own imagination!

Let's create a ripple of success, income, and IMPACT!

LISA COBBLE

EXCEED COACHING

EXCEED-COACHING.CO.UK

Chapter 14

Why Not?!

By Lisa Cobble

It's January 2021. My business is set up, I have two clients, I am getting involved with more in my day job to feel like I am contributing, while I wait for IT development time. I have been in my current corporate role for over 2 years, worked for my current boss for almost 5 years and I am happily running my own business alongside. I am comfortable.

One night, I am sitting on my sofa with my family, and I casually check my work phone, which I do on and off to make sure I am being responsive where I can, as I have a global role. There is an invite from a man who's name I recognise but have not had a lot to do with. He was my counterpart in Engineering's ex-boss. The invite indicated he had spoken to my counterpart and my current boss and would like to speak to me about my career aspirations. I was immediately excited!

Let me say that up until then, I had not expected there to be roles available in such a strange time in the world. In a global pandemic, home working, in a place where keeping going and being grateful that I could continue with a job and run my business, was a blessing.

So, I decided to ask my boss what was going on. He explained there was a role available, similar to another I was aware of, and that I should look at it.

A lot about the other job was not what I wanted. It was data, dashboards, rhythms, routines, pressure. I saw that and I instantly thought 'no'. I was happy, I could juggle what I had. Why change that? Why disrupt what I had built? I wanted to move to my own company full time as soon as I could. I was going to gracefully decline. My boss told me 'just listen, see what it is, be open to it'. I wasn't convinced.

The day for the career discussion arrived. I met with the man I had barely worked with, I listened, I took notes and I saw lots of similarities to a time in my past when I had worked in a sales support role. Although the terms were different, it felt familiar. It was also in a different area of the business that I found exciting, interesting, and honestly right up my street! I liked the man I was talking to. Some of my yes indicators started to twinkle.

I needed more information, so I spoke to the lady who was leaving the role, and I still saw a lot of 'danger' in the words I wrote down - exposure, know your data, present to upper leadership. A lot was scary. A lot worried me and was not what I wanted.

And then I started to get romanced. I would be a 'Director' in a huge worldwide organisation, I would work at a level I believed I was capable of, I would be in an area of business that I saw as the future, that I had touched in my past. Others had recommended me...I felt like the river of fate was flowing fast and sweeping me along with it. Like I somehow was having an out of body experience, watching myself being taken towards what I should do. As if everyone else was right.

I spoke to a colleague that I didn't know so well, to get a more level headed view, to slow the pace of the river. After a discussion he told me I was comfortable, I had my slippers on. At 42 I was too young to have my slippers on (metaphorically, I have mostly been wearing nothing but slippers since March 2020!). It struck me he was right. I instantly knew I had more to give, and I should not waste the opportunity. My colleague also asked me to consider three scenarios - how would I feel in 6 months if I a) didn't apply b) applied and didn't get it c) applied and got it.

From that discussion, I knew I should apply. I let the course of the river sweep me further towards the new role. I confirmed I was interested.

I hadn't asked many questions about the role. I watched some videos. I was happy to throw my hat in and be considered. I was still being level headed at this point, not allowing excitement to creep in, but being very aware of how I was flowing fast in that direction.

I had four interviews with various members of the team. I got a really good feeling about the people I would work with. One HR team member who interviewed me, already knew me from my STEM volunteering and we already had a fabulous relationship. During my final discussion with my potential new boss, we had talked about other roles I had been in and people I had worked with. About how I had handled difficult situations. About other work experiences managing processes, tools, change and business improvement.

It felt good to know I had such a strong history.

And then, a few weeks later, as I was wondering if anything would come of it, a call came in while I was on lunch. It was my potential new boss and I had missed him! So I messaged him straight back, typing as fast as I could!

A few minutes later he called me and said, “You are the one. You are the best!”. And I burst. I was so excited, honoured, happy and grateful. I listened as he told me that he had spoken to others from my previous roles, everyone who had interviewed me, it was all good. And I was the chosen one.

AMAZING!!!
So I was set. Things were put in motion and I would start to transition on 1st April. This is the thing about moving roles within an organisation, there never appears to be a clear cut off! So, as excited as I was, I agreed.

I would work from home permanently, I could keep the routines I had developed (to a degree) and I would gradually ramp up in the new role. There was no need to 'say goodbye' to anyone and I could stay in touch. I was one message away. Perfect!

And so it began. Easter gave me a small buffer of time to 'swap' mindsets and focus in on the thing that mattered, the transition. I started a new mind map, new box folders, new favourites, and new files. It was exciting. I spent some quiet time mapping out all the new team members so that I could recognise who they were, and where they fit when I spoke with them, I was invited to many 'intro' meetings. It was fun to meet back up with some colleagues from my past. And as the news started to spread in the organisation, there was nothing but praise and congratulations.

Now, one month in, I can share with you my reflections on this whole experience.

I was adamant at the start that I did not want the role, that I would not like it and I didn't have the skills. Those who had recommended me were not right, they didn't know me, and it would not suit me. I am not good at data crunching, at presenting data to upper management who know better than me, I had my own business to run, and I was happily 'getting on with things'.

And then the 'slippers on' conversation came up. It was a light bulb moment. In the words of a wonderful connection of mine, I wasn't done yet! It was such a release.

A few weeks into the role, when things started to 'settle', I sat back and looked at the raging river of activities that had brought me to that point. Recommendations from people I had worked with past and present, the connections back to previous roles, the sparks of interest I have always had for this area of the business, the excitement of being approached to apply, the belief that others had in me that I could do it, that I was perfect for the role and that it was right up my street.

And I realised, I felt like I was home.

I have never moved into a role and felt so secure, so safe and so welcomed. It is like a dream.

And I chose the word 'romanced' earlier to share with you something I tell my clients to avoid. 'Don't let fancy titles, bonuses and perks, romance you into a role you do not want'. I fought the urge to jump at it for all of those material things. And when I stripped the role of those sparkly things, I still felt like I should give myself a shot. And I have never been happier to have done that. Why ignore everyone else around me, why look a gift horse in the mouth, WHY NOT?!

LYNNE PAGE

TRAVEL PA

LYNNEPAGETRAVEL-PA.CO.UK

Chapter 15

From Bank Clerk to Travel Agent

By Lynne Page

At 16 I got a job at a local High Street bank until I decided what I really wanted to do as a career. Little did I know that it would take me over 30 years to realise that was not the direction in which I wanted my future career to head.

I had done various different roles in the bank. But the last couple of years became tougher and more challenging for me. This resulted in me being extremely ill with my mental health and having to take a lot of time off work.

I have lived with depression and anxiety for many years, going back to my mid-twenties. It wasn't discussed as much back then in the 1990s, resulting in me not getting the support I so desperately needed. After seeking help from my GP, on each occasion I was referred for counselling and prescribed anti-depressants. I have found that I really need to 'click' with a counsellor and trust them, in order to build a relationship and trust them enough to open up. Unfortunately, that didn't happen until I sought therapy privately a couple of years ago. I finally found a Clinical Psychologist that made me feel at ease and I was happy to talk openly to him.

After our initial session, we discussed what sort of therapy I would be having, starting with Compassion Focused Therapy. This is used to treat problems associated with shame, self-criticism, and self-hate, which can be features of anxiety and depression. It can help you develop, and work with, experiences of inner warmth, safeness and soothing, via compassion and self-compassion. It became clear that I needed to have more compassion towards myself, not others. I needed to be kinder to myself and stop thinking of myself as a burden to my husband and family. I had to stop the feelings of guilt about having a mental illness.

Upon hearing this, I stated that there had been times when I thought everyone would be better off without me as I am such a burden and strain. It would have been easy just to take all my medication in one go and not wake up in the morning. That was so hard to admit and say out loud to another person. Even now whilst writing the words I feel emotional. I could not do that to the people I love. They mean the world to me. It made me realise I had to push those dark thoughts away and be grateful to have a loving, hardworking, supportive husband, and a family who love me unconditionally.

After getting all of this off my chest to my therapist, he explained we would be going through Acceptance and Commitment Therapy (A.C.T). It is split into three different categories: Mindfulness, Acceptance and Values. We started with mindfulness, which I still practice to this day.

I made myself comfortable in the chair with my feet on the floor (this helps you to feel grounded), I shut my eyes and just listened to his voice. His soothing tones told me to be aware of my surroundings, the sounds, the feeling of the chair, the taste in my mouth, the smell of the room. If I had other thoughts going on or my mind wandered, he assured me that was fine. I was to take notice of my breathing, every time my lungs fill with air I then breathe out and they are then empty, and I don't even have to try, it just happens automatically. And the whole time his calming voice is saying that it's OK for my mind to wander, just come back to my breathing...in and out...in and out.

I was so relaxed I have no idea how long this went on for, I could quite easily have fallen asleep. I heard him say for me to start becoming aware of the sounds, the feel, the smell, and the taste and then to open my eyes and take in my surroundings.

At the next session we looked at Acceptance. One of the analogies he gave me was to see my anxious/negative thoughts as leaves on a stream, acknowledge they are there, but don't pick them out of the stream. Just let them float by. He explained that the part of my brain where anxiety is (our flight or fight mode if you like) is in overdrive and the part where my self-confidence is, he likened to a weak, spindly muscle in need of a bootcamp session.

We then moved on to Values, which involved me identifying what it is in life that is important to me and gives my life meaning and purpose. It was at this point I knew, that after being away from work for a significant amount of time, I had been working in a very toxic environment and I knew I didn't want to go back there. It was a proper 'light bulb' moment. Having identified this, I needed to think about what direction I wanted my life and career to progress towards. I had so much to think about and discuss with my husband. But at least it was something positive.

I spoke to my husband, Gary, and chatted to my family and friends about my decision to leave my secure job of 30 years. It was a massive decision but as soon as I'd made it, I could feel the weight lifting off my shoulders. It felt right. Now I needed a plan for my future. What did I want to do? What would I enjoy doing? How would I handle my anxiety through all of this?

My brother suggested, as I loved to travel so much and was always happy passing on advice and recommendations, that I look at a franchise and retrain as a travel agent. I would be able to work from home and be my own boss, which in turn could help with my anxiety.

I started to do my research into different homeworking franchises and did my pros and cons list with Gary. I noticed that the company I had been booking my holidays with for the last few years offered franchises for homeworkers. Cue the second 'light bulb' moment! I hadn't realised this was an option. A company I knew and trusted. I contacted them and had a chat about all the options, I explained my circumstances and about my anxiety. They were happy to answer as many questions as I had flying around my head.

That was it. The perfect solution. Gary and I decided to use our savings for the franchise, and I typed out my letter of resignation, giving the bank a month's notice.

The countdown was on to my new beginning.

As a catastrophic thinker, my next hurdle was being brave enough to travel to Head Office and stay for 5 days for my Travel Academy training. Although I wasn't going back to the bank, my anxiety levels were still high. This was a big deal. It would have involved over an hour on the train, then the tube, then another train journey and then trying to find my hotel and training headquarters. Gary said he would drive me down there the night before, so I didn't have to go on the train, he would stay with me for the first night and then return to pick me up when the training was finished.

I really enjoyed my training, although I had so much to learn. I was finally starting to feel excited about my future. This all happened in the latter part of 2019. I started setting up my business ready to launch in January 2020. Even my catastrophic brain could not have predicted a global pandemic though. Not the best time to start in the travel industry.

So the world came to a standstill. Nobody could travel. What was I going to do now? Six months previously I would probably have had a panic attack, closed my curtains, and got into bed for a week. Not now though. I took the opportunity to go on as many training webinars as I could with tour operators and suppliers and learn as much as possible.

I did something I had never done before and joined networking groups on Zoom. I wouldn't have been brave enough to do networking in person at that point, but I felt quite safe on Zoom. I also signed up to do some business and social media courses and workshops, as I had so much to learn about running a business.

I took it upon myself to contact our local newspaper to ask if they ever featured a travel blog. The editor quickly came back to me and asked if I would like to do a travel column. I snapped her hand off and now have a regular column every four weeks. This reignited my passion for writing, which I find very cathartic.

While I was taking time off from the bank, I started writing a mental health blog, because I was suffering with insomnia. I had so many things racing around my head, it helped to write them down. I put them into a blog, hoping it might help at least one person who read it.

Leaving my old job and starting my own business has opened up a whole new world to me. I am stronger and more confident. Gary even says I am like the old Lynne but more amazing. As well as the people that have supported me along the way I have also met new friends and colleagues, who cheer me on at every step. The words that have been used to describe me over the last year are 'Resilient' and 'Transformation'.

I am so excited for what the future holds. Bring it on!

PHOENIX MADLEY

VISIONARY HEART

VISIONARY-HEART.COM

Chapter 16

The Archetype

By Phoenix Madley

Hardship cannot find the heart that is open to the changes of life. It cannot truly damage what's within. The heart is concealed with a lock and key. Only you are the master of the lock. When you open yourself to the wonders of the world, you take that wonder in as yours, and find the place for it which no one else can touch.

You have not lost yourself because the person inside of you was already found. It was found the moment you set foot into this very birth. Hardship may mould you into a shape that you have not conceived of. But then the task is to take that which you have become by hardship and return to your own vision of yourself. You can find yourself in the task of life. A simple moment. You can find yourself in the discussions with others, the moment you wake to set gazing eyes upon the day. We are gazing eyes you see through. We see through all. Archangel Michael.

I felt like life was against me. And I thought, what could I have possibly done to deserve this? As it happens, life did not have a personal vendetta. Life does not choose to be against you. You get to view things through the filter of your perceptions, beliefs, and attitudes. There I was, left with facing myself. Left with what I felt was nothing. In some ways, you have to lose it all, to find it all. As in build from the ground up. That the place of nothing is the place of possibility.

My life was in tatters after having to give up my rented flat due to illness. That took an ugly form of a nervous breakdown in 2011. I was not able to hold down my job. And moving back home, although I rebuilt my life there, was a big blow to me. I was living on a small handout the Government provided. My mind had crashed. Everything I had dumped in there over the years came up to be seen and validated.

Who was I? What was my purpose? The part of me that had put everyone's needs first, who had committed suicide many years before the breakdown. There I was, believing I had done enough inner work. However, as I had learnt, inner work never really ends. At that time, what also came up was the part of me that had all the answers. And also, the part of me that was strong, confident, and courageous. Those qualities to me felt so distant.

It is easy to feel like a nobody. Unworthy, unloved. Not being seen and heard. Do you know that feeling? I had nothing left to put into life. My juice and zest had gone. When life presents a trauma, we often think we lose certain qualities within ourselves. We perceive those things as being taken away by people, or the challenges we have faced. Paradoxically it is those same challenging events that allow us to embrace those qualities. Or keep them further at bay.

In each challenge or obstacle, we can either confirm our worth, or we can validate why we don't matter. How would our lives be if we embraced the qualities we believe we don't have? For me, I discovered many of my lost qualities in Archetypes. Archetypes are universally recognised. They are Gods, Goddesses, Angels, magical beings, and symbols. At the same time, Archetypes are deep parts of the psyche. They are the unreachable parts of the unconscious. They contain all the qualities we believe we don't have. And in those traumatic times in our lives Archetypes can present themselves. That part of unconsciousness in ourselves comes forth to help us. Archangel Michael represented my lost confidence, courage and strength. In many ways, he made me realise I was those things.

Question? What things in your life represent the inner qualities in you that you feel are missing? And can you incorporate those things into your outer life to help put you in touch with those aspects of yourself? Maybe it's a statue, or a picture or some magical being.

I would spend copious amounts of time doing automatic writing. As in typing questions and waiting for the answers, which I then would write down. Or I would ask the questions in my mind's eye. Answers came through me about the deeper workings of life, giving me hope and inspiration. Sometimes answers would pop up many days later, when not expected. Sometimes it was like a sensation that I interpreted as words. Or sometimes it was like an inner voice that was my own. Yet it felt deeper, using words in my vocabulary.

At that terrible time in my life I would meet people in town, trading Oracle card readings for a chat over a cup of coffee. The connection to others was nourishing to me. I would talk to the homeless and those addicted to drugs. I would listen to people's problems and issues. I would let people open up to me. In all of that, I found we all shared common humanity. We all have hopes, dreams, and aspirations. We all have insecurities and what we don't show to the world. In some way, this gave me the space to find the time I needed to focus on rebuilding my life back then.

Things have radically changed since then. I run a non-profit business, I work fulltime. I am a co-author. I have publications in a magazine, and my life is abundant and full. I still face life's twists and turns. Yet who doesn't confront all those things?

I found the attitude we take on, who we believe we are, becomes the platform for our lives and how we view things. It's not that you have to be positive. It's about how you communicate with the negative feelings, emotions and thoughts that are there.

Feelings and emotions are sacred messengers of what you need and want. You then learn that they have a purpose. Even the negative feelings and emotions are worthy of being felt, seen, and heard. It's then that how you see yourself changes. You can fail, feel sad, and still be enough. You can also experience hardship and challenges and still be a worthy person.

Often, we were taught when growing up, that experiencing those certain emotions made us bad and wrong. Or that life in its challenging moments meant we were less. It's then these self-evaluations restrict us to a world where we don't see or act upon those opportunities in our environment. Life is already there, waiting for you to embrace it, waiting for you to scoop up what is on offer. Changing how you see yourself changes how you face things; alongside the risks and opportunities you are willing to take. All I can say is go for it. Many people will come and go in your life, and many situations will change. There will also be joy, success, and beautiful things that you will experience. Equally, there will be loss, failure, and sorrow as well. And there will be you - facing all of it!

Exercise: Maybe you would like to partake in a reflective moment for yourself, in order to take an insightful journey, to trust what comes up for you. What qualities do you feel are missing in your life right now? What age were you when you gave those qualities up? What was happening in your life when you decided you couldn't cope? That those inner qualities were not enough? Or maybe you decided that those qualities were too much to have, from fear of being judged. What things did you decide about yourself as a result of that situation? By not having those qualities in your life. By choosing to give those qualities up, what have you given up in life? What chances have you missed out on? What opportunities? What is so scary about having those qualities?

Would you be willing to embrace those qualities again if you could take that younger self and tell her/him all the things she/he is, that she/he has come to be in the world? That those qualities are a panacea! That boundless opportunities await to bring those qualities to. How would her/his life be different with those things present? And what actions would you be willing to take now?

RITA PRESTON

RITAPRESTONSVIEWS.COM

RITAPRESTON.COM

Chapter 17

Wither an Adventure

By Rita Preston

The year 2020 changed the world. Thinking of one person who did not experience change from the global pandemic is nigh to impossible.

Our office was running full-tilt and suddenly I received a text from a colleague firmly compelling me to stay home because of my asthmatic lungs. The Shutdown occurred in the middle of our busy (income tax) season in the United States.

Life changed for all of us at some point in the early months. Wither and mope? Make a new life? What did you do?

Sitting still was not an option for me. I needed 'something' to do. For personal satisfaction, for stress relief, for growth. My retired husband, an active disabled veteran, has been my cheerleader!

On a lark, I signed up for a discounted writing course advertised on social media. The adventure was afoot! Writing courses to sharpen my long-brushed-aside skills as a scribe. My blog, begun in 2012 covering a myriad of topics, has a small following. Staying home pushed me to put my quill to better use.

Unbeknownst to me, a dear friend, an author in her own right, was being led to launch a collaborative faith-based book series. Hearing her call, I leapt at the chance.

One year post Shutdown, I am now a co-author working on the third volume of our series, while crunching numbers in the tax office owned for over 30 years by another cherished friend. As I write this chapter for yet another collaborative series, led by a new friend 'across the pond' (as my late dad used to refer to Great Britain), I cannot help but be amazed at the passage of time. The changes in our world at large and our own personal abodes.

Over one year later from that imperative plea for me to stay home, our office has been in full swing again. I eat lunch at my desk, but instead of just working through lunch, or surfing the internet, I pull out my lime green clipboard with my 'list' and my drafts, and I read. I rarely edit there. Just read. (Yes, sometimes I surf the 'net!) Now that winter is fading away, I may take a short walk. I may walk to the convenience store and simply browse. I find myself refreshed after this break and my hours on the job are less stressful and pass with less effort. One mini vacation every day!

Another change for me at my day job in taxes: I used to stress internally over having cut my hours following a broken hip several years ago. I realised my body slowed down and my employer, my friend, talked with me regarding the hours I would find most comfortable.

I started back with afternoons and have tried to stick with that, going in earlier and staying later when necessary. That used to stress me out, horrendously. I felt guilty for not pulling the extra-long days I had pursued for decades.

Since returning to the office last summer (fortunately I missed only a couple of months pandemically speaking) I no longer carry the guilt as I approach the office door.

My colleagues work their hours and I work mine. I am trying to keep mornings for me. Coffee. Time with my husband, retired for nine years now from his civilian job. Time with our varying small zoo of pets. Time to read. Time to write. Time to attend to appointments from haircuts to chiropractic adjustments and now, acupuncture!

I am blessed to be able to do this. Not everyone can, but my colleagues who have joined our staff over the last 15 years or so can handle things very well. I am proud of them and confident in them. I have worked over 30 years in this profession with my dear friend. We have been blessed with relatively small turnover in staffing, and all have ended up as women (we didn't plan for an all-female office, it just happened that way). We cover for each other when there is a family concern or health issue. Family first. We each contribute to our churches and community organisations to the best of our abilities through volunteer service. We are women of faith and we value teamwork. I could not have asked God to find a better work environment than this!

We have shared the loss of loved ones through the years at the office, from siblings and parents to children and grandchildren. We have cried and prayed together. We continued our prayers throughout the pandemic.

My classes continue and I have added more to my roster. I carry a notebook and jot ideas. I take photographs (another hobby) and thank the inventor of the digital age for saving me fortunes in film developing costs! The difference now is that I jot a note or thought about the photo before the day's end. There may be a story hiding in those pixels!

I have been in touch with a couple of photographers for whom I've previously modelled, and discussions are underway regarding the need for camera time. People of all walks, occupations, genders, faiths, and wealth are feeling cooped up like chickens in a hen house. We want out. We want to be the social beings we naturally are.

I think we have all learned that social media is not as social as we first thought. It has its place to be sure, but it is no substitute for being around other living beings, interacting, hearing laughter that has not been digitised, and hugging others. Even if you were not a hugger before the pandemic, I bet most people are cherishing their first hugs after a very long year.

One strange occurrence of note for myself during the past year: all this free time that was available and Hubby and I rode less on our Harley-Davidson™ Ultra Classic than in years prior. We stayed home, even though the open road was a prime location for social distancing. Groceries are still being delivered; I think that essential service spoiled me.

Santa Claus delivered a new toy for Hubby during our pandemic-style Christmas. Santa works miracles sometimes. It is a 1970s Ed Roth chopper style trike (motorcycle) that will be easier for Hubby to ride, as Agent Orange induced peripheral neuropathy badgers the nerves in his feet. Ours is certainly not the first veteran household to switch from 2-wheels to 3-wheels. We are keeping the Harley for now, and I pray continually for a miracle that would allow Hubby to cruise down the open road again on just two wheels.

Realistically, I have had to accept we will never ride the Harley to Alaska, pulling a little bike trailer with camping gear, for the adventure we always talked about. Too many things have interrupted those plans. From my broken hip to various commitments. Hope springs eternal that we can take the trike, or perhaps tow the bike/trike behind our ancient motorhome (picture the one owned by 'Cousin Eddy' in the movie 'National Lampoon's Christmas Vacation').

The pandemic shutdown allowed me to look at desires I tucked away decades ago. My high school English teacher counselled my parents and me most wisely: *Rita can write, but writers traditionally starve. Keep writing as a hobby and find something from which to earn a living.* My chosen university major? Foreign language and international studies; I said I 'hated' math and just look at the calculating occupation I chose! Never say never!

The year is 2021, something we dreamed about as children watching science fiction television shows (dare I mention Black & White TV?). We imagined flying cars and living in space.

Humankind has pulled off the feat of a few humans living on the International Space Station. We have sent robotic scouts to Mars. We can connect in seconds for live video with family and friends around the globe.

Even with the massive surge of technological advances, the planet came to a screeching halt by a tiny little germ: Covid-19. Apparently, humankind has a lot to learn. We still can't cure the common cold, let alone this highly contagious variant of the same family of sickness 'bugs'. As the warm weather arrives, I hear motorcycles go past the office and our home outside of town. My husband, doing his best not to wither as well, has been tinkering with our 'toys'. We anticipate the wind on our faces. My notebook will be in my travel pack with my camera. Adventure beckons!

Whether or not there is a shutdown, we must not wither! I will nourish my spirit. I shall do my best to look out for Hubby, my colleagues, my family, and my friends. I will write. Perhaps we may even meet down the road. Look for us at rest stops (we need many more stops than we did years ago) and national parks!

SARAH ROSS

YOUR REASON TO BREATHE

YOURREASONTOBREATHE.COM

Chapter 18

My One-Way Ticket Out

By Sarah Ross

The corporate world had destroyed me; I was burnt out. It didn't happen overnight, but I hit rock bottom. Continuous stress from travelling and looking after 50 countries across the globe, working exceptionally long hours and at times delivering the work of three people, had triggered chronic migraines. For at least 25 days a month, my head would feel like there was a burning ice pick stuck deep inside it. I would pray that the pain, nausea, and partial loss of sight would stop quickly. My only relief would be a dark, cold silent room. For months, I would wake up and hope that today would be a good day, and that I would be pain free, even if it were only for a few hours.

Yet during those days of agony alone in my room, my inner bully, the loud nasty voice inside my head which I knew so well, was getting the better of me. Telling me in the darkness, over and over, "You're a failure. You're disappointing everyone. Why would anyone want you? Look at yourself", and "You're not good enough".

My self-esteem was at rock bottom, my relationship had fallen apart, and my health was a mess. This stress and the constant migraines ultimately led to me accepting redundancy.

As I looked at my severance cheque, I took it as a metaphor for my life. I didn't have anything left to live for, and so on my 37th birthday, I decided that I would not see my 38th. I bought a one-way ticket to Vietnam and intended to die there. I even chose my "Expiry Date" - January 31, 2015. I decided to give myself six more months to live so I could see the people I wanted to see and do the things I still wanted to do. And I would spend the last three months of my life volunteering with disabled children in Vietnam.

Room Five at the orphanage was a room unlike any I had ever spent time in before. It's where 20 children who were left alone by the world lived. More than half of them were abandoned by their parents. They often had a medical condition their parents couldn't afford to care for or chose not to bother with. There was a minimal level of care for them. They were given food, shelter, clothing, and medical care. They were safe. Yet, there was something powerful about Room Five that I just couldn't ignore, so I became their regular volunteer for three months.

For eight hours a day, five days a week, my purpose was to care for those forgotten children. And as the days and months passed, my spirit for life found its way back to me. I painted their nails, blew up balloons and sharpened their pencils. I played with their pet rocks with them and bought socks and hats for them, both items which are rarely donated.

We built Lego towers and destroyed them, always with a laugh or cheer. When we were allowed, weather permitting, we went outside so they could breathe fresh air, and I did what I could to keep them away from rats and open sewage drains.

The culture shock was what I needed at the lowest point in my life. Rather than trying to bring the luxuries I was accustomed to into their lives for a short period of time, as volunteers we were encouraged to find sustainable ways to make their lifestyle better with what was available locally. Finding solutions to things like drying clothes and cloth diapers without a machine when it's raining outside, or how to keep 20 children clean without a bathtub, silenced that nasty voice in my head, my thoughts began to change and slowly I started to come out of the haze of depression.

As my time in Vietnam included December, I decided to spend my final Christmas bringing Santa Claus to the orphanage. On Christmas Day I walked around the centre visiting all 180 of the orphans. Each child getting chocolate or a lollipop and most grabbing my beard playfully before hiding. The pure and innocent interactions with the children that day, sparked a renewed sense of purpose.

One of the little girls in the orphanage was incredibly ill, and we were told that she wasn't expected to live through the night, so we should say our goodbyes before leaving for the day.

As I leant over the metal crib, still dressed as Santa, this poorly little girl, no more than 4 years old, raised her hand and touched my beard. She was fighting for every breath, even though to those around her, she had nothing to live for. She had been ill from birth, abandoned by her family, and would never have gone to school, as disability is not looked on favourably in her culture.

While looking in her eyes and watching her struggle to breathe, I questioned my own plan. In comparison to this beautiful little soul, I had lived an abundant life and the possibilities for my future would have been everything she could ever have imagined. Travel, education, and family. Why was I giving up when there was so much more I could give and do in the world? In a beautiful shared moment, she taught me that I still had a "Reason to Breathe", and I chose to live.

I left the room that afternoon in a daze. I was at a crossroads and I wasn't sure what I should do next. For so long, I had been focused on ending my life and experiencing the "lasts" in my life, the last plane trip, my last immigration queue, my last Christmas. I had gotten myself to this point, yet I had no idea how to change the direction of my life. I needed to ask someone for help, and that was something that I had never really done before, too afraid of looking weak or disappointing people when they realised I was struggling.

I got back to my room that night and sat on my bed. I really didn't know who to ask. Still not wanting my friends or family to know how bad things were, I saw a book on the table. It was from a speaker training I had attended as part of my bucket list. One of L.A.'s top acting coaches had called me out for not being authentic when I spoke on stage but said his classes could help me. When he and I parted that day, I swore I would never be in the same room as him again. I hated him. Yet the inscription he had written in the book for me made me reach out to him.

"The bigger the dream, the better the life"

Desperate to change my life and break through the burnout cycle, I went with the unknown and signed up for his acting classes. I had no idea how far outside my comfort zone this would take me, but I needed an environment that was the polar opposite to the corporate life I had been living.

In fact, the iconic song from Disney's *Frozen*, "Let it Go", about a girl making a stand for who she really is and not hiding anymore, would become my ticket back to the real world. As I spread my arms wide in a beautiful old theatre in Rome, and let the air fill my lungs to hit that powerful chorus, it felt like I was breaking free from all the chains that had bound and smothered me for so long. My voice was finally alive and strong again.

Since that day, I've continued to push my boundaries; I've done stand-up comedy based on my own life story, partied at the Oscars, and walked the red carpet at an Italian film festival. But more importantly, I've become a multi award-winning International Speaker empowering others to make decisions in difficult situations. Using my stories and experiences to help those burying their pain and burning out to know that there was someone on their side. Someone who would support them, listen to them, and help them to be the best version of themselves.

I will never forget the gift that beautiful little soul gave me on that Christmas Day in Vietnam. She saved my life and helped me find my “Reason to Breathe”. The following months that I spent in Room Five, gave me a renewed sense of hope and joy for life that nowhere else in the world could possibly have shown me. And I’ve been back four times since - twice more as Father Christmas - to give back to that special place that taught me how to smile and laugh again!

STEPHANIE LETHBRIDGE

C S PLANNERS

CSPLANNERS.COM

Chapter 19

The Impossible is Possible

By Stefanie Lethbridge

February 2020 was the month I decided to free myself from the haunting memories of my past. I was knocked down so hard this month that I wasn't sure if I could get back up again. Every time I would close my eyes, I would relive my past traumas. I was exhausted, hurt, and confused on what to do. My name is Stefanie, I am the Co-Founder of CS Planners and I am going to take you on a journey of these memories and what completely changed my life to being free!

When I was 13 years old, my biological father got me extremely drunk and gave me a pill that caused me to black out. I was haunted by the memory of my dad standing over me laughing while I was laying on the floor sick and struggling to breathe. I remember thinking that I was going to die, and he just stood there and took pictures. This memory of my father hurting me and not doing anything to help me was so painful that I would sometimes wish that I would have ended up dead that night. I tried to tell myself to not think about this memory for years as it caused me a lot of anxiety. For years I let this memory control my life and it held me back from feeling free.

After living through the trauma and abuse my dad caused me, my mom struggling to support us as a single mom, and older men sexually assaulting me, I thought I was done living through the hardest part of my life. I met my husband at the age of 14 and he was the person that made me feel like all of my struggles were behind me. We were happy, in love, and our family started to grow. Just when we thought everything was going right for us, on February 23, 2016, our son passed away.

I still remember how it all happened. On February 8, 2016 in the middle of the night, I woke up and saw blood everywhere. We rushed to the hospital and the doctors told me that my baby would be fine and that everything I was experiencing was normal. I held onto those words and trusted that there was a chance my baby boy would be okay. The more that time went on, the worse it got. I was in and out of the hospital for weeks, just praying that he would be okay.

There was one morning when I saw a beam of sunlight come through my living room window in just the right way to make an angel shadow. At that moment, there was something telling me that that would be the day I would lose my son, and I was right.

On February 23, I went into the hospital and my water broke. The pain was worse than labour because I didn't have contractions, it was just constant pain. Not only did I have to live through the pain of going through labour, but I knew that when he came out, he would be still.

I developed a blood clot in my uterus that pushed him out and I carried the guilt of feeling like it was my fault for years. I felt like my body failed. After delivering my son, I had the opportunity to hold him and spend time with him. The moment I held my son, still, completely changed my life. I remember wishing for him to be here, but at the same time I was grateful to just be holding onto him. It was a moment that will stick in my head forever because it reminds me that life is too short. He didn't get a chance to walk, talk, breathe or any of the things that people take for granted. I will admit that I was also one of those people for a really long time.

My husband Jake completely changed my life. He made me believe that the impossible IS possible. We ended up going to visit fertility doctors and we were constantly told that my body would never allow me to carry a baby full term. This was really hard for me to accept and added on to the guilt I was already carrying. I remember my husband saying to me, "doctors say we can't have kids naturally, but watch us. If you want to have a baby, nothing will get in our way".

It was hard, but we decided to remain optimistic and decided to still try for another baby. I knew that I was going to become unstoppable and that's when everything changed! I was finally able to carry a baby full term and we now have a healthy baby girl who is 3 years old.

The moment I held my daughter for the first time, I knew that the impossible was possible. I am still told that I can't carry a baby full term and doctors are shocked when they hear me tell them that despite what they believe, I was still able to deliver a healthy baby girl. They are always telling me that they are shocked and that I am lucky. It made me believe that if I could have kids when Doctors told me that I couldn't, what else could I do? I made it my mission to start a business so I could have the freedom to spend more time with my daughter and husband. If my little boy taught me anything, it's to enjoy every minute of life because you have no idea when your last day will be.

While I was on maternity leave, I struggled with the idea of going back to a 9-5 job. I kept thinking about how hard it was to have my daughter and I just wanted to be able to spend as much time with her as I could. That's when I decided to start a business. Within the first week of launching I was able to get my first client! I grew very quickly, but I decided to still go back to my 9-5 job because I felt the pressure of other people's opinions.

I had a business, full time job, and a little baby at home who was up all night. To say I was exhausted was an understatement.

I was so grateful when Chelsea, someone I worked with at my corporate job, offered to help. That was the beginning of our business partnership.

In February 2020 I wasn't able to sleep because every time I closed my eyes, I was reliving these memories and feeling the guilt and shame. I still blamed myself for the loss of my son, and I also started reliving the memory of my dad on my 13th birthday, which caused me a lot of anxiety. I completely broke down and my business partner, Chelsea, not only took over all of the work but helped me become free from these memories. I tried therapy and it didn't work for me which added more stress and anxiety. Chelsea helped me master my mind so I didn't let my past control my future, and taught me different strategies that allowed me to control my anxiety. These lessons allowed me to finally become free.

The hardest part was getting rid of the guilt that I felt. To help with the guilt, I focused on the affirmation "I am phenomenal". On the car ride to work each day, I would be thinking about that affirmation, and to be honest, I didn't believe it at all. The more I listened to it, the more it became real to me. All of a sudden, I would be sitting there and the words "I am phenomenal" would randomly pop into my head. Eventually, I started to believe it.

Throughout my biggest struggles I took each one as a lesson. Right after my son was born, my husband asked me "what good is here that I cannot see?"

That question forced me to think about being grateful for those little things in life. The fact that I have some incredibly supportive friends, family, and husband was at the top of my list.

Sometimes it's when you appreciate the little things in life that you realize the true beauty in any situation.

Looking back, I wish I would have given myself some advice right from the beginning. The advice I wish I knew then was to take each day as they come and know that the hard time will pass. Enjoy the little things in life because if you don't, you could be wasting the rest of your life worried or stressed. I hope this advice will inspire you if you are going through a hard time right now.

I am now living my dream life and I want to empower others to do the same. I am on a mission to help heal your mind and soul so that you can start living your dream life! I want to teach people that the impossible IS possible even if life knocks you down.

SUSAN TOTMAN

VIRTUAL BUSINESS PRO

VIRTUALBUSINESSPRO.COM

Chapter 20

Eliminate the Box

By Susan M. Totman

All of my adult life, I'd been careful. As a person with a plethora of serious health issues over the years, there was always a little voice in the back of my head saying, "What if...?" Living in that sort of a shell became a way of life. No risk taking or chances. Do what needs to be done, but do it safely. For years and years, I considered spontaneity and taking risks, foolish chances that could risk the children's future in some way, especially if it meant they may be without their Mom or Dad. Never once in all that time did I consider what putting myself inside that box was doing to my own psyche.

When we became parents, it was the ultimate gift to us. We had lost several babies in the process of trying to have a child, so being a Mom - a good and responsible Mom - became my primary purpose and focus. I was dedicated and enchanted by these little beings we were blessed with.

As our children grew up and moved on to lives of their own, building their own universe, I remained inside that "box", rarely venturing outside the status quo.

Interestingly, they have always seemed to observe the world as having no box, because that is what we taught them, contrary to how we were actually behaving with ourselves.

Are you seeing the problem yet? Yeah, me too. I encouraged my children to do what they dreamed and live what they love, which is great, but in the process, I never let myself do the same.

In August of 2014, we had an opportunity to spend a day with my brother Steve and sister-in-law in Bar Harbor, Maine. Bar Harbor is about 87 miles from our home, on the rocky coast of Maine. As we were discussing how to spend the day, we decided to rent some scooters and travel to Cadillac Mountain, a short distance away.

Now it may seem silly, but to me, driving anything on two wheels by myself was HUGE. I had ridden on the back of motorcycles, but never driven anything by myself on two wheels. Not only did I choose to drive my own, but I didn't rent the helmet either. I threw caution to the wind - literally! My husband thought I'd gone bonkers - he was shocked.

It was a gorgeous day, sunny and beautiful. We rode to the mountain, climbing the winding road with some very tight curves when suddenly, I failed to negotiate a curve.

I did not drop it or crash, thankfully. I managed somehow to hold it upright, turn and very slowly continue forward until I regained traction on the road, and off we went again, all the way to the top and back down again.

We rode for hours and I was as red as a lobster when we were done, or in true Maine fashion, I should say lobstah!

That day was the catalyst for future events. My husband had an opportunity to buy a little Suzuki Savage (thumper) motorcycle for a great price. Knowing how much I had enjoyed the day on the scooter “in the wind”, he truly thought buying the motorcycle would be the motivation I needed to get my motorcycle endorsement and really learn to ride. What he didn’t anticipate was that I was still stuck in the box. It would sit for another year before that motivation had a fire lit under it.

The following August, a beautiful friend of mine, Kelley, invited me to lunch. She was not doing well, battling cancer that had spread far and wide, but no matter how hard it was, she continued to smile and tell everyone else it was going to be OK.

That day, as we chatted, she told me something I will never forget. She said, “Stop putting off your dreams. Do the scary things, the fun things. Don’t waste it.” What I did not know in that moment was that in about two weeks, she would be gone from this world. That was the last time we spoke other than chatting on Facebook. She was 35 years old. She didn’t waste even a second of it. Despite years of intense treatment and horrific symptoms, she refused to believe that giving up was an option.

Just a couple of days after Kelley passed, I had an opportunity to get the motorcycle training course for half price. After our discussion, I felt that this was serendipitous and that it was not only the right time, but THE time. Time to let loose on the boundaries I’d set so long ago and allow myself to just enjoy.

So I enrolled in the course (for my son Joshua as well), had my husband register the Suzuki and get it ready to ride, and off we went to learn to ride.

To say it was different than I thought it would be is an understatement. Riding a motorcycle - even a little 250 as they had in the class - is VERY different than riding a scooter! The class was a two-day event, with Day 1 being horribly hot at nearly 100 degrees F, and Day 2 was hot, but also rained off and on. Suffice it to say that weather-wise, it was a miserable couple of days, but being on the motorcycles and moving kept us busy and going.

The physical process of getting my license was not terribly tough. I struggled with a couple of areas, such as figure 8 and curves, but as soon as I understood that I needed to look where I wanted to go and the bike would follow, I was hooked. The instructor instantly saw it as soon as it all clicked for me and he was grinning from ear to ear, delighted.

Despite my initial trepidation, Joshua and I easily passed the course. He was quite experienced on dirt bikes and such, so for him, it was much different. I had no such experiences - except the scooter (eye roll) I soon realised however, that my knowledge of driving standard vehicles was going to turn out to be advantageous.

Once I passed, I was free to ride my motorcycle anywhere I wanted to. I rode up and down our road for a few days, getting familiar with it. Then one day my son Matt said, “I'll follow you in case you have trouble.” I hopped on and headed for the main route, driving slowly initially…the rest, as they say, is history!

Five and a half years later, I have approximately 20,000 miles under my belt as a driver, all of it in Maine to date, mostly due to health challenges that make it difficult for me to travel too far. We don't mind staying local to our region and thoroughly enjoy being in the wind, knees in the breeze, or however one wants to phrase it.

Over the course of my life, I have experienced nothing as freeing as riding my bike, in the open air, with random fragrance in the air (yes, even the manure as we ride by the local farms and fields) as we pass through the natural beauty of this region, giving us an immense appreciation for our surroundings.

Our current goal is to get a toy hauler camper in the next year or two that will allow us to travel with the bikes and have a place to stay at the same time. Riding them long distance is not a possibility with ongoing health challenges, so it's the perfect solution to really see the entire country (and beyond) and enjoy some real time with each other as we move into our silver years. We have been married for 36 years this year, together 38. We have worked hard all of our lives and it's time to relax a little, but not too much! There are so many exciting experiences left to live. Fortunately, I am able to work from anywhere working virtually, so this is a very real aspiration that we can look forward to.

This year I also intend to jump out of a perfectly good airplane, going skydiving just because I can. Am I scared? No, I'm terrified! That said, I am excited to push my own boundaries even further and eliminate the box altogether.

My advice to others is not to allow the box to ever be created. We pigeonhole ourselves into spaces because of our own unrealistic expectations that are often far too rigid, and often downright impossible to achieve and maintain anyway. Be willing to expand your horizons, even if you're scared. Push yourself outside your comfort zone. In fact, give yourself permission to make your comfort zone limitless.

UNA ROSE

UNIQUE NEW ADVENTURE

UNIQUENEWADVENTURE.COM

Chapter 21

Window of Opportunity

By Una Rose

How many times have you heard this phrase "Window of Opportunity"? For a promotion, for a new job, for meeting someone, starting that project. The list goes on.

For me, this phrase will forever stay in my mind for baby number two. It was abbreviated to WOO, and to this day it makes me both smile and cry.

I always wanted to be a mother, even though over the years I was convinced I was not going to be able to. Dreams turning in to nightmares as I was so convinced of that fact.

Myself and my husband met later in life, I was 35 and he was 37, and within a year and a half we were married. Within 6 months of marriage I was expecting our first child.

I enjoyed the pregnancy, I loved the movements, the comparing the size to vegetables, I was ready for the responsibility and for life changing forever, and I got used to my ever-expanding body. I was grateful for this blessing.

I often say it is truly amazing a woman and man can create a baby by two things you can't see with the naked eye.

He arrived and all was wonderful, a healthy boy, my dream of a waterbirth, and yes life changed forever. This is really grown up - bringing life into the world is as serious as it gets.

I settled into parenthood, the ups and downs of breastfeeding, sleepless nights, loss of independence and so much more. I made copious videos, took thousands of pictures, and kept everything he made.

Time went on and I wanted another baby, surely he or she would be great company for my son. I am one of five and my husband is one of three, so we agreed to adding to our wonderful family. We didn't see the road ahead - no one did.

WOO took over our lives. Calendars, apps, sticks, temperatures, seeing babies EVERYWHERE, and everyone asking, 'So what about number two?' - a question I loathed as each time I was asked I cried inside.

Two years later and we were still trying, and still fixated on the WOO. The fun and joy were removed. The spontaneity was gone. It was all dictated by dates and temperatures and stress from me, I know that now.

But we kept going and then one day I knew something wasn't right, I felt sore, I was eating LOADS, my app said I missed a period and of course my mind went into overdrive. Could we be?

Like anyone trying for a baby you keep this all to yourself, I know this is changing, but back then it was not talked about until sadly it needed to be.

I bought a test and did it at home, smiling when the lines showed that I was indeed pregnant. I was 6 weeks pregnant. We decided to say nothing for a week or two. We were of course thrilled, and I already knew the due date. I was having dreams about the children playing together in the garden.

We invited my parents and brother to our house for lunch one day and declared the news. They already knew due to the changes in my body - my chest especially. It felt wonderful to say it out loud, as I am sure my parents were thinking it but would never have said anything.

Things changed drastically after that lunch, within less than a week something wasn't right this time. I had been having spotting for a few days and convinced myself all was OK. I Googled the life out of my symptoms until finally I was in work and started to panic. It was a Friday, and I discovered the Early Pregnancy Unit (EPU), did tests. This place was never even in my mind.

Thanks to one of my sisters, who made a call to her consultant, we were seen earlier than if we didn't have that connection.

Off we went to the EPU, the waiting room was full of couples all in for the same reason. I saw posters, 1 in 4 pregnancies end in miscarriage. This word had never passed my lips before. I was frightened and I held my husbands' hand tightly.

Our time came to go in, and it is a day that will never leave me. The room was clinical, of course, with the typical stirrup chair for me to lose all sense of dignity in. The most amazing lady with such a kind manner came in, and explained what she needed to do. Up I got onto the chair, and for the second time in my life I was examined internally - the first time was in Baghdad, but that is another story.

There was silence, concentrated faces and shuffling of feet. The screen was turned around so we could see it, and all was explained. It was all so matter of fact but that is a day that rocked my world. I have no idea what was said as my ears were ringing, and I had tears in my eyes. The baby due on November 30th was no more, the name was gone, the birthdays were gone, the company for our son was gone in that second and my heart broke. We were left alone, and I howled like a wolf and we held each other as if we were drowning.

We pulled ourselves together and had to walk past pregnant women as we left. I called my parents from the car and could hardly speak to them. They were devastated for us.

We got back home, and I didn't want to see or speak to anyone, only my family knew, but slowly I told people.

To get through it I let myself go down a very black hole. I let myself go deep and cried for a month. I wrote my feelings down. I took time off work, but I didn't hide the reason as it was my way of dealing with it. I visited websites, joined groups, and blamed myself for a long time. I had no idea it was so common as no one talks about it, and I know why. I hugged my son too much, I am sure.

I will never forget my pregnancy number two.

We tried again. The WOO reappeared when I was ready, and I got pregnant again. This time I did the test in work as I didn't want the memory in the house. Sadly, I needed to recontact the EPU a second time and I was seen by the same lady. I was less scared this time as I knew the truth before it was confirmed. My second miscarriage in a few months.

I decided to leave number two for a while. I couldn't mentally cope, and I began to look at my son as an only child. I'd always said if it wasn't possible, I would accept it.

We booked ourselves in to the Fertility Clinic for a discussion, and after that we both agreed if it didn't happen naturally over the course of 6 months, I would not be going down the IVF route.

I had been through enough and I was not prepared to put myself through any more physical and mental torture.

For both our sakes we literally then didn't discuss anything about baby number two, and I deleted the apps and unsubscribed from emails.

My 40th birthday came around and the three of us headed off to Majorca for a fun filled time. We relaxed for the first time in months and had a ball.

Unbeknownst to me I came home expecting, something I discovered a few weeks after we returned. We went to the EPU very early in this pregnancy as I wanted to check all was OK. The same consultant didn't lead the examination - they don't do more than two, for obvious reasons.

This time we heard wonderful news and heard a beating heart. The same consultant was in the room, she handed me a tissue and I squeezed her hand tightly without saying a word. She knows and we are so happy. I breathe again. I cry.

This pregnancy was the opposite of my first as I was tense and anxious that something may happen. It had been a living hell, so we shared the joyful news early with our families. In the end all was well and a healthy boy was born in the same water bath as his brother, and we became a family of four.

I am sharing this for others in the same situation - keep the faith. It is such an emotional rollercoaster. I hate what happened, but it happened.

Today I feel blessed with my boys and one day I will explain what happened and why there are four years between them!

Nature can be cruel, but it can also provide priceless gifts.

Epilogue

Thank you for purchasing a copy of this book. I hope you were able to find strength by reading the stories of others and sharing their experiences. If you are currently going through any of the experiences you've read within this book, please know that there is light at the end of the tunnel.

Look at the reflections from the Authors in here and try and find some answers for your own situation.

If you would like to share your own story, please do contact us for details on how you can take part in first becoming a Contributing Article Writer for our global magazine, MO2VATE and subsequently, Volume Two of this anthology.

If you enjoyed this book, we would love a review on Amazon.

Thank you again for taking the time to read our Authors' journeys.

Preview: Revival: Women Embracing Their Superpowers (Volume One)

'Living Life on Purpose' by Olive Pellington

"When you know you were born for more than where you currently are and you know that you were put on this earth for a purpose, life begins to change. Somehow it seems like suddenly the sun just got a lot brighter. Truth be told, if we had been noticing the subtle changes, the slight nudges in course correction, we would have seen the beautiful morphing shades of the sunrise. But because we allow 'life' to get in the way, the nudges become shoves and the changes become cliff hangers. So, like any other insane entrepreneur, I decided to grow my wings on the way down. Thankfully, like an eagle, I don't stay down for long."

To purchase this book, click here:
https://amzn.to/2Rq1Jn8

Preview: Revival: Women Embracing Their Superpowers (Volume Two)

"Little Girl Lost – On the Other Side' by Alison Wombwell

"July 2019 – the month and year that will forever stay with me. It was when my whole life changed. I had just received a diagnosis of Autism. I was Thirty-four years old.

At a time when I should have felt relieved and at peace finally understanding who I was, I did not. In fact, I felt incredibly low. I felt like everything that I thought I was, was a lie. It was like someone had said, you are autistic now, you can take your mask off, you can be yourself. I did not know how to be myself.

To purchase this book, click here:
https://amzn.to/34O6pq2

About the book creator

Sharon Brown moved to the West Midlands in 2003 from Glasgow. She worked her way up through various positions and industries and finally started her own events agency in 2015 after a long career in the corporate world. A Qualified Project, Event and Marketing Professional, Sharon seized an opportunity to get online with her business in 2018 after realizing a new way of working was needed.

Revival Sanctuary, a global community for women in business was born after some serious soul searching and market research within the women's networking space. Sharon has always understood that in order to get anywhere, it's far easier and quicker to do this with the right team of people and so the Revival ethos of Collaboration over Competition has been embraced and encouraged throughout the community.

Within this space, new projects have evolved allowing members to work together and to make an income, raise their profiles and increase their brand visibility. One of these projects is MO2VATE Magazine which is a global business bible, aimed at micro and small business owners. The beauty of this magazine lies in the article writers who are all business owners so the value is immense to all who subscribe to it.

Further projects include The Speakers Index, which is a public speakers directory and The Book Chief, a Publishing House which caters and encourages business owners to 'Ignite Their Writing' by publishing either their own book or a collaborative one. This book is published by The Book Chief.

Services

The Book Chief Publishing House | Ignite Your Writing

www.thebookchief.com

A Publishing House aimed at turning small business owners into credible authors with affordable and creative options for all.

MO2VATE Magazine | The Winning Formula

www.mo2vatemagazine.com

MO2VATE Magazine is a business magazine with a global reach. The magazine is produced, written and published by small business owners with the aim of raising their profiles through exposure, reach and building their authority.

The Speakers Index Directory | Amplify Your Voice

www.thespeakersindex.com

THE SPEAKERS INDEX is for anyone who practices public speaking and wishes to get in front of the right people to allow them to raise their profiles with a better opportunity of being seen and booked.

Revival Sanctuary | For Women in Business

www.revivalsanctuary.co.uk

REVIVAL SANCTUARY is an Exclusive Private Membership Club for women in business. It attracts women who are comfortable in their own skin, supportive of other women and those willing to empower and collaborate with each other.

Printed in Great Britain
by Amazon